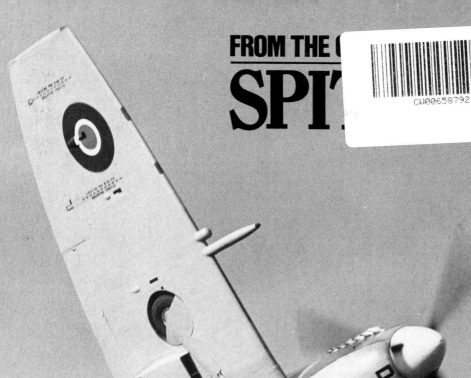
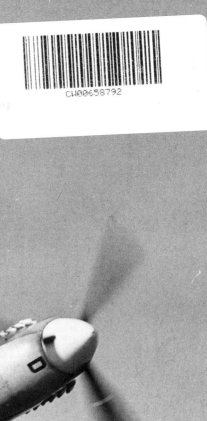

FROM THE C...
SPIT

CW00658792

FROM THE COCKPIT

SPITFIRE

Wg Cdr T.F. Neil DFC*, AFC, AE

LONDON

IAN ALLAN LTD

specialtypress

First published 1990

ISBN 0 7110 1918 5

Published in the United Kingdom by
Ian Allan Ltd, Shepperton, Surrey;
and printed by Ian Allan Printing Ltd
at their works at Coombelands in
Runnymede, England

Published in the United States of
America by Speciality Press,
PO Box 338, 123 North Second Street,
Stillwater, MN 55082 USA

Catalogue of Congress Number:
Available on Demand

Half title and this page:
**The Shuttleworth Trust Spitfire
— a bit of a hybrid but closer than
most to the original — which is a
'clipped, cropped and clapped'
Mk V. Apart from the ejector
exhausts, the similarity is almost
exact. This aircraft has a clipped
universal 'C' wing plus cannons
and a gunsight, which most
refurbished Spitfires do not. It
also sports the newer windscreen
and a de Havilland metal
airscrew.**
Jeff Ball and Air Portraits

Previous page:
**A beautiful aircraft — the Mk XI.
One of my favourite Spits to fly, it
was always painted blue and had
masses of fuel but no armament.
A photographic reconnaissance
(PR) aircraft, surprisingly it did
not have a pressurised cockpit,
although the Mk X, which was
almost identical to the XI, did.**
Aeroplane Monthly/RAFM

*Front cover photograph by
Allan Burney*

Rear cover:
**Photographed by courtesy of the
Battle of Britain Memorial Flight
this view shows a pilot settling
himself into a Spitfire cockpit.**
Chris Shaw

Rear cover (inset):
A portrait of the author.
RAF Museum

CONTENTS

FOREWORD

Spitfire! What memories the name evokes!

The Spit was a unique aircraft — unique in efficiency and performance, unique in design and grace of line; unique, too, in character, name and docility.

Produced initially at a time when the Royal Air Force was still flying fabric-skinned biplane fighters mounting two machine guns, with its single wing, all-metal construction and battery of eight Brownings, it was positively space-age, a 'hot ship' in popular parlance, to be flown only by a special breed of supermen who wore the new oxygen masks which gave them a quite specious 'hard-men' anonymity and who were later permitted to wear their uniform tunics with the top button undone.

I saw my first Spitfire, in the flesh so to speak, when sitting on the grass at the Hendon Air Display of 1936. I was 15 at the time and its brief appearance, with the equally new Hawker Hurri-cane, produced moments of breathless excitement. Less than four years later, I would be shoe-horned apprehensively into a Spitfire cockpit, having never flown anything more modern than a Hawker Hart biplane at flying training school, and told to 'get on with it'.

Below:
Sheep in wolf's clothing — the prototype Spitfire K5054 in its first Service camouflage. *Flight*

Below right:
The Spitfire F21, 22 and 24s were all biggish, heavy aircraft with a redesigned wing and tabbed ailerons which changed the type's flying characteristics quite markedly. However, with the introduction of jet aircraft towards the end of the war, interest in the Spitfire waned and they were flown mainly in overseas theatres and by the Auxiliary squadrons up to and beyond 1950. Illustrated are Mk 21s flown by No 600 Squadron in 1948. *Flight 21694*

Thereafter, I flew the Spitfire at various times and in many places and conditions throughout the war and, having had the good fortune to survive and move into the test-piloting business, was enabled to fly all but several of the 24 marks of Spit which were produced in the 11 years between 1935 and 1946.

For any writer, the saga of the Spitfire represents an embarrassment of riches; so much has been said and written on the subject that to repeat a mass of statistics or provide an anthology of war experiences would, quite properly, be seen as mere duplication. Moreover, it is clearly an undertaking far beyond the compass of 80 pages to deal adequately with the 50 or so variants of Spitfire produced during and immediately after World War 2.

For these reasons, I have chosen to focus my remarks on two marks of Spitfire which saw operational service in 1942-43: the Mk V, of which there were more produced than any other variant, and the Mk XII, which, although few in number, were rather special as they were the first type of Spitfire to be fitted with the Rolls-Royce Griffon engine.

In 1942, Jeffrey Quill, the test pilot largely responsible for the development of the aircraft, made a most apposite remark when describing the Spitfire, which even then was becoming larger than life in the nation's perception and esteem.

He said: 'The Spitfire is a plain, straightforward piece of mechanical engineering, differing little, other than in size and shape, from the Forth Bridge or the humblest motor-car.'

And, of course, he was right. The aircraft, being a production-line item, was built to calculated strengths and tolerances and, quite capable of being bent or even broken, could be a good or not-so-good example of its type. In the same way as there are 'Friday afternoon' cars today, there were 'Friday afternoon' Spitfires in war, aircraft which proved to be wayward, perversely awkward, even downright jinxed.

This, then, is less about the glamorous Spitfire of popular imagination, around which so much folklore had been invented and repeated, and more about the average Spit, how it measured up and behaved when flown by those equally average young men who were obliged to use it in battle.

INTRODUCTION

At the end of August 1942, I was posted to command No 41 (Fighter) Squadron, then stationed at RAF Llanbedr, near Harlech in Wales. The squadron was equipped with Spitfire Mk Vbs and operated mainly from Llanbedr and occasionally, when circumstances demanded, from Tangmere and its satellite airfield West Hampnett — now the Goodwood motor-racing circuit in Sussex.

Needless to say I was delighted. My new command, one of the oldest and most famous squadrons in the RAF, was well known to me as it had fought with great distinction from Hornchurch, in Essex, during the Battle of Britain, at a time when I was flying Hurricanes from nearby North Weald.

With bright expectations of personal fame and fortune, I was a little discouraged to learn on arrival that I was the unit's fourth commanding officer in as many months, my predecessor having been killed two weeks earlier over Dieppe when on his first operational sortie.

The second unexpected jolt occurred when I suffered an engine failure on my second flight in the Spitfire 'specially selected' for me by the squadron engineer officer, causing me to cogitate not only on the fallibility of engineer officers but of Spitfire Mk Vs in general.

Early in 1943, the unit was re-equipped with Mk XIIs, an event not without incident, thereafter being employed operationally in several roles and from many airfields in the South of England.

But of these and other aircraft in detail, more in a moment.

Below:
19 Squadron airborne before the war — four 'vics' of three, a formation much used even during the early part of the Battle of Britain.

PLACE: **RAF Woodvale**

DATE: **November 1942**

There were hints of another night attack on Liverpool, and in expectation of a raid, six of us in Spitfires had flown across from Llanbedr to Woodvale, near Southport. Single-engined fighter squadrons at that stage of the war were still regarded as day-and-night interceptors, although there were already in being many specialist night-fighter units flying Beaufighters and Mosquitos.

Each pilot of No 41 Squadron flew a minimum of one hour per month at night, just to keep his hand in. The prospects of intercepting anything, though, were remote. Without airborne radar, the Spit was almost useless in the dark; even in the most favourable conditions of moonlight and weather, the pilot could see next to nothing in the air.

Even so, the citizens of Britain, who were constantly having bombs dropped on their heads,

Below:
Part of No 9 Group Fighter Command's area in 1942, showing the locations of Liverpool, Woodvale and Llanbedr.

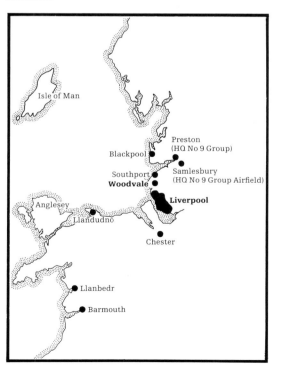

liked to hear the sound of their own aircraft and in this respect our involvement was justified; our Spitfires, being Mk Vs, had a distinctive whistle when flying, not unlike a note of a Pan's pipe, and could be recognised even when they could not be seen. Later on, the Mk IXs and others lost this endearing characteristic, which, for most of us, was a sad development.

Having arrived at Woodvale in the afternoon, we learned that we were to become involved in a 'fighter night', an arrangement in which fighters were sent off and layered at 1,000ft intervals in the area of a possible target and at the likely height of the bombers. I had taken part in many such exercises in the past and had had limited success in England towards the end of 1940 and rather better luck in Malta a year later, where the weather and the searchlights were rather more helpful.

Thus forewarned, we made ready.

It is sometime after 10pm, very dark and the weather indifferent. There are enemy aircraft to the south of us, apparently, but no one knows precisely for which target they are heading. After a routine but comprehensive briefing, it is decided that we should position ourselves — just in case!

The first to go, I sign the authorisation book for my own flight and authorise those of the other five pilots. I then scan the Form 700 of EB-V, my personal aircraft and the one in which I had had the engine problem three months earlier and which now is fitted with a new Merlin. I note that the engine has completed 46hr — nicely run in — although the airframe is much older — 170hr. No major difficulties though during the last several flights, everything signed for and correct, my flight from Llanbedr the same afternoon constituting the statutory night-flying test.

Out then into the darkness. Blackness everywhere, a raw damp wind and unseen cloud. In the near distance, a small nodding torchbeam, carefully shielded in the blackout — my crew, guiding me.

My Spitfire looms, the duck-egg blue of its pointed spinner dimly visible in the darkness. I am carrying my helmet, gloves, mask and radio lead but my parachute with its attached dinghy is in the cockpit. Before the days of dinghies, I used to prefer my parachute being laid out on the tailplane but now the dinghy is too cumbersome, so into the cockpit it goes — with everyone treading on it!

I step on to the wingroot and into the dark cockpit and switch on the so-called floodlights which cast a muted pink glow from left to right over my instruments — which are luminous anyway — leaving much of the cockpit in shadow. There is the heavy fragrance of dope and petrol. On either side, the wingtips are lost in darkness, my navigation lights not being switched on, but a grey smudge at face level indicates that my rigger is by the trolley-ack (trolley-ack — battery cart used for starting up), my fitter standing alongside me to help with the straps.

I attach the dinghy lead to my Mae West then sort out my parachute harness, clipping the metal ends into the circular release box on my tummy. After that it's my Sutton harness — left shoulder, right leg, right shoulder, left leg — all gathered together and the split-pin securely in place. I free the harness with the toggle on my right-hand side, bend forward, then lean back and feel the lock click into place. Fine!

Now my helmet, oxygen tube and radio plug — all fitted and in position. Finally, my goggles, then my gloves — all three pairs at the ready but on my left hand only for the moment.

I switch on the oxygen, then cast an eye to the needles on the 'contents' and 'flow' dials. After which, a quick check for delivery; I block off the tube and after some moments, feel the oxygen pulse against my fingers. Everything okay!

I wriggle in my seat, anxious to manoeuvre the steel bottle of the dinghy away from the bones of my backside, and nod to my fitter who lifts the lolling flap to my cockpit and clips it into place. After which, with a farewell touch to my shoulder, he steps down into the darkness and ducks under the wing to take charge of the chocks which block the two wheels of my Spit. I'm safely in and tied down! Now for it!

First, up with the two levers which turn on the fuel — all 85gal of it. I unscrew the ki-gas primer and squirt — one, two, three, four squidgy strokes, the petrol from a leaking gland cool on my ungloved fingers. Then, up with the two magneto switches to my left and two more fingers of my right hand on the starter and booster buttons. I nod automatically to my crew and move the throttle a fraction. A slight jerk as a single blade of the airscrew moves around unseen in the darkness accompanied by the familiar clank of the reduction gear. A cough and a shudder. Another. And yet a third before the engine bursts into life with a blast of air around my head and the tang of exhaust fumes in my masked face. Momentarily, the Spit lifts against the chocks and I sense rather than see my rigger struggling down on my right-hand side, removing the heavy plug of the starter trolley and buttoning in place the covering flap.

The engine settles down to a steady 1,200 revs, warming up. The coolant temperature is off the clock still and the oil temperature five degrees, or thereabouts. On its small upright gauge, the oil pressure registers a steady 70lb.

I scan the cockpit. Everything all right, or so it seems. I wait, one eye on the coolant temperature, my instruments flicking into life as my aircraft battery and generator take over. In front, the artificial horizon starts to quiver as its gyroscope begins to spin. My Spit is stretching itself like a cat, flexing its claws and muscles. I switch on my radio and after some moments 'huff' into my transmitter. In front and to my left, the single green eye which signifies my wheels are down and locked, stares back at me unwinkingly. I wait. And watch. Outside the dimly-lit cockpit, everywhere is bleak November blackness.

The coolant temperature rises — slowly, like a watched kettle taking an age to boil. Soon, though, it is 60° and sufficient for run-up. I check the radiator flap, which is open, the lever on my left side fully forward.

I am aware that my crew hate these run-ups, particularly in winter, as they normally have to drape themselves over the tailplane to prevent the aircraft tipping forward. They are relieved, therefore, when I do not motion them to the rear; having given the engine a good work-out several hours earlier, there is no need for me to beat it to death yet again.

I run-up gently to 0lb boost, watching the temperature and pressures, exercise the Rotol airscrew twice throughout its pitch range of 35° and

Below:

Spitfires were designed as day and night interceptors and were employed occasionally as night fighters until about the end of 1942. As such they were pretty poor: visibility from the cockpit was indifferent, particularly at night, and the aircraft itself waywardly frisky on the ground, resulting in a higher-than-average accident rate. This Mk V is taking off at dusk; had it been dark you wouldn't have seen it — naturally!

screw the friction-nut on the throttle assembly until it is nicely tight.

Then the mag switches: I switch them off one at a time and feel the engine droop fractionally, the exhausts flaring minutely as though in protest. The revs drop a trifle, too, but well within the 50 the engine is allowed. As I close the throttle, a shower of incandescent particles shoot from the exhaust stubs and the Spitfire lolls back from the chocks. Everything in order. I bend down and set the compass — carefully, because it is difficult to see low down and in shadow behind the control column — then set the direction indicator equally carefully. Half-deciding to switch on my gunsight, I have second thoughts — plenty of time for that! Oh, and the pitot-head heater! I switch it on, profoundly relieved — not the sort of weather to forget *that*!

Satisfied, I lean back in my seat, reduce the intensity of light in my cockpit to the barest minimum, and think about moving off. Everything is pitch black apart from a curving line of tiny lights

marking the perimeter track. Finally, to enable the duty pilot at the end of the runway to see me coming, I turn on my navigation lights — green on my right wing, red to my left, and white behind me. They will be off in the air, of course; no one flew with nav lights burning in wartime — or if they did, not for long!

I wave away the chocks, move slowly on to the perimeter track and begin to jink — in so far as the narrow concrete strip will allow — Spits being *brutes* to taxi, the nose stretching so far out in front. But I can't make too much of a meal of getting to the end of the runway as the engine heats up very quickly even with the rad flap fully open and I can't afford to let the temperature get beyond 100°, otherwise the engine will boil during take-off, spout steam and corruption all over everywhere and frighten me to death. So, I continue more rapidly, the brakes hissing like cobras and the engine favouring me with pungent snarls as I negotiate each bend.

The main runway approaches, its lights only a little brighter than the perimeter track markers, and a green light clicks brilliantly in my direction — clear on to the runway, the duty pilot is telling me. I move ahead carefully, lining up exactly on the undulating row of lights stretching away into the distance. No other lights anywhere — no outer or inner markers, nothing. Just a single trail vanishing into an endless bowl of darkness. I stop and note with satisfaction that my compass and DI record exactly the direction of the runway. All right so far!

My Spit is trembling and eager to be off as I check my cockpit for the umpteenth time. Elevator trim — one division nose down; rudder — full right on the bias; mixture — forget it; pitch — fully fine; flaps — up; fuel — both tanks levers up and contents checked; harness and hood — locked and secure. I feel around with questioning fingers. A final glance at the radiator temperature, which is close to 100°, making sure that the rad flap is open. After which, I move forward carefully, kicking the rudder.

I never attempt to raise the tail on a Spit but just allow the aircraft to sort itself out from the sitting position, comfortable in the knowledge that after a few moments I shall be able to see ahead. Meanwhile, in the tail-down attitude, it is important at night to steer a course which is exactly parallel to the lights which are about to stream past on my left. I advance the throttle to get her running straight and we set off at a fast trot.

In moments we are rolling nicely down the centreline at which point I open up firmly to 6lb boost, kicking the rudder to keep the mettlesome creature on course. Then, in a firm movement, my throttle right up to the gate so that with 9lb showing on the gauge, my Spit is fairly flying down the runway and clawing forward into the black void beyond.

In seconds she is rising — touching — finally lifting away cleanly, the runway lights falling away downwards and disappearing astern. In front and all around, nothing but endless, frightening blackness, the exhausts of the raging engine cherry-red with snarling effort, everything tight and vibrating.

Up wheels! I change hands on the control column and move the lever in the undercarriage box down a little, a half-inch to the left, then up and into its notch. The single green light disappears, the rotating wheels shaking violently until I stop them with a touch of brake, after which — just for several moments during which I wonder if the hydraulic system is going to work — a minor 'clump' and a red

Left:
A Sector Control Room at work, similar to many throughout the country in 1942-43.
RAF Museum (RAFM) U114

light appears. In position and locked! I throttle back a trifle, note the slight deceleration and reduction in commotion up front, then, with 150 on the clock, climb away. The altimeter registers 500ft with the needle moving quickly around the dial. I am up and climbing into the blackest of caverns, the magenta and red of the angry exhaust stubs fading away to a friendly, faintly flaring pink, the occasional white-hot fragment of something or other whirling away into dark oblivion behind.

The best climbing speed of a Spit low down is about 180. Half instrument flying but with part of one eye cocked to my left, watching for the line of the horizon, I throttle back to about 6lb boost — no need to break my neck — reduce to 2,650revs and allow the aircraft to take up its proper climbing attitude. After that, as arranged, I press button 'B' on my radio and call Sector.

Neil: 'Hello Inkpen. This is Mitor 14. Airborne and climbing to patrol line. Any trade?'
Sector: 'Mitor 14. This is Inkpen. Nothing at the moment. Call when in position.'

I acknowledge, and that is that.

Well into the climb and ascending through 5,000ft, I am in and out of cloud for a time, the aircraft rocking and buffeting as it ploughs through the murk, which I only recognise as vapour when the meagre light in my cockpit takes on a faintly diffused aspect. Soon, though, I am on top and in clear air, an indistinct but discernible horizon all around.

I scan my instruments. Oil pressure 65lb, oil temperature coming up to 60°, coolant temperature 85° — I slip the radiator flap into the half-way minimum drag position. I reckon I am out to sea somewhere west of Liverpool and make a rate-one turn to the left which will bring me back over land. I can see nothing of the city below nor even the coastline or river, there being no moon and the stars being singularly unhelpful.

Between my knees, the compass needle swings slowly in its bowl and the DI turns gently in its circular window. I adjust the revs slightly to find a more comfortable setting and note that I am lifting through 11,000ft. Two other members of 41 are calling Sector and climbing up below me. All we need now are Germans!

It takes me about 20min to climb unhurriedly to 24,000ft and having arrived there, I throttle back to 0lb boost and reduce the revs to 2,000 — no point in wasting fuel. The ASI shows a little under 200mph, although I am aware that I am going much quicker in true airspeed terms — about 270 in fact. I decide to check my position.

Neil: 'Inkpen, this is Mitor 14. At patrol height now. Where am I precisely?'

Sector: 'Mitor 14, we have you 10 miles south of "X" '. The controller gives the codeword for Liverpool. 'Flash your weapon.'

I fish around to my right in the dark cockpit and locate the switch which operates my IFF. After which:

Sector: 'Mitor 14, your position confirmed as 10 miles south of "X" '
Neil: 'Any trade?'
Sector: 'Not a sausage!'

Controllers like to appear human now and then.

Having 'unflashed' my weapon, I settle down to the mind-boggling boredom of flying in wide figures-of-eight at 24,000ft. I reduce my cockpit lights to zero so that I fly entirely on the luminosity of my dials, switch on my gunsight, dimming the fiery graticules so that they are barely visible, and turn my gunbuttons to 'FIRE', just for the hell of it. The engine exhausts, a dull pink now with tiny rippling ice-blue flames, still have the effect of almost wholly destroying my night vision.

Thirty minutes pass. Then 45. Finally 50. Round and round. Back and forth. Oh, for a German or two! The many pointers on the dials in front of me comfortably static or wandering about with controlled regularity. Everything exactly right.

By this time a numbing cold is beginning to bite — my fingers especially. I shift uncomfortably on my dinghy-pack and check my oxygen flow. Five miles below, Greater Liverpool goes about its silent business in stygian darkness. Not a single light anywhere — in England, even. Had they heard my whistle, I wonder? Were they even aware?

Suddenly, there appears a dull splurge of something far beneath and, as I watch, tiny pools of light ripple across the underside of the clouds like mice tripping across a ceiling. Searchlights! From my towering position, I look down like God and watch them besport themselves for a time then think it prudent to enquire.

Neil: 'Inkpen. This is Mitor 14. I have searchlights below me. Anything happening?'
Sector: 'Mitor 14. Stand by.'

Then after a long pause:

Sector: 'Mitor 14, one, possibly two bogeys approaching from the south. Angels uncertain at present. Maintain your present position.'

Instantly on the qui vive, I acknowledge the message and set about preparing my cockpit — I check my fuel state, readjust the intensity of light in my gunsight, ensure — for about the fifth time — that

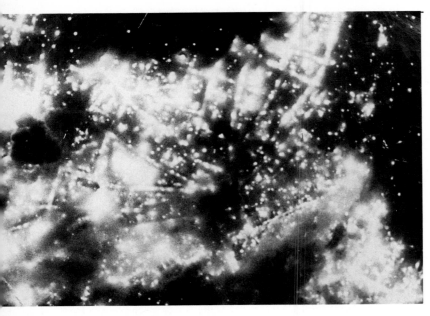

my guns are on 'FIRE', increase my revs to 2,850, and generally smarten myself up. My exhausts exuding a flaring pink glow in the blackness ahead, I find myself wishing that I could open the hood to get a cleared view, but at 220 indicated it is immovable, as I am well aware, so there is no point even trying. Then, impatiently:

Neil: 'Inkpen. This is Mitor 14. Any further news?'
Sector: 'Mitor 14. One bogey now twenty/two-zero miles south of you, confirmed at angels one-five. Maintain your present height and position.'

A flash of irritation. So what! — do they or don't they want me to intercept? If they do, what am I doing waltzing about at 24,000ft? There are two other Spits below me I know, but . . . ! I make my point in a terse sentence but am told to stay where I am. Wriggling in my seat with impatience, I note that I have been

airborne just over an hour, so that I haven't much time to spare. I peer downwards. Come on! Get on with it!

Minutes pass. I circle endlessly. The blighter should be here by now. Far below, small discs of light wander about like bunches of lemmings against the undersides of the cloud. Searching. Clearly undecided. Then, all at once — *concentrating*!

I am in a steepish turn and standing on my starboard wingtip when, directly below me and silhouetted briefly against the lightened cloud, the tiniest of tadpoles that is a twin-engined aircraft, drifts into view for the briefest of moments before melting into dark obscurity. The bogey! Or was it? More than a mile beneath, recognition is out of the question. Immediately:

Neil: 'Inkpen. Mitor 14. Tallyho! I have an aircraft directly below me. Going down to investigate.'

Without waiting to be authorised or even forbidden, I fling my aircraft into a dive, beside myself with excitement.

A brief silence. Then a voice, slightly on edge and clearly apprehensive:

Sector: 'Mitor 14. Proceed with caution. Other friendly aircraft in your area and bogey not yet positively identified.'

Caution? What rot! There is an aircraft down there just *waiting* to be shot down! I am barely 22 years of age and caution is almost a foreign word.

My Spitfire is falling like a stone now, its controls tight with hissing speed. In seconds, 350 indicated, the needle on the ASI moving purposefully around the dial, everything drumming and trembling with exulting anticipation.

Tilted steeply downward, thousands of feet hurtle by. Then, aware that my Spit is beginning to run away with me on a very dark night, I pull out very circumspectly, feeling 'g' drag at my body and sight and thankful that my artificial horizon has not toppled as the result of my ham-fisted gyrations. I note that I am at about 17,000ft, going like the clappers, heading due west and out to sea. The searchlights far astern of me now, in every direction a blank, impenetrable wall of darkness. And of the bogey — *nothing*! Not an exhaust flare, a flicker or a glimpse.

My pulse returns to normal as reaction sets in. Inkpen and I compare notes. The controller below is a bit plaintive and clearly uncertain as to what exactly is going on — although he does not admit as much — and eventually asks me to 'flash my weapon'. I do so, heading rapidly in the direction of Dublin meanwhile, and after a seemingly endless, suspenseful silence, I am imformed that I am six miles south of 'Y' — the codeword for Llandudno. I have been airborne 72min, apparently, and am advised to return to base without delay. Faintly indignant, I ask what has become of the bogey, but no one seems to know.

Completely deflated, I check my fuel — about 28gal remaining, sufficient for 30min flying at most. I throttle back to 0lb boost and reduce revs to 2,000. After which, I make a rate-one turn to the right and opt for assistance.

Neil: 'Inkpen. This is Mitor 14. Request fix and vector for base.'

Sector: 'Mitor 14, this is Inkpen. Transmit for fix.'

I acknowledge and leave my radio on 'transmit' for 10sec so that the three direction-finding stations in the Sector can triangulate my position, then:

Sector: 'Mitor 14, we have you four miles north-east of "Y". Vector zero-seven-four degrees, distance 46 miles.'

I acknowledge the information by repeating it and turn for home.

On my way back to Woodvale, I begin to lose height gradually, watching the various instruments on my dashboard record my descent. My airspeed up again to 260 and my engine cooling, I close the radiator flap to prevent the temperature falling below 85°. No sign of icing around the cockpit, plenty of oxygen still and about 22gal of fuel in the bottom tank — everything fine. I increase revs to 2,400 and reduce boost to −2lb. Ahead and in every direction, nothing but inky blackness.

After about five minutes, I am given another vector, zero-seven-eight. I change direction slightly and note that I am at 10,000ft and descending rapidly with 280 on the clock.

Then cloud — a lot of harsh corrugated bumps and a sudden awareness of mist. I switch on my navigation lights briefly and have my suspicions confirmed when the red and green lights produce ghostly glows. After which I am back in the clear again, everything tight and hissing with speed.

Now 4,000ft; no mountains around here but I mustn't overshoot and drift into the lower hills of the Pennines. I throttle back further to −4lb boost and allow the speed to fall. Soon my ASI is showing 240 and I am down to 2,000ft.

I am thinking about a further vector from control when I happen to see the faint line of the flare-path at Woodvale. Spot on! I circle the airfield at a comfortable distance then join the circuit, switching on my nav lights, something I would not dream of doing had the enemy been close at hand.

At 1,000ft, I turn crosswind knowing full well that Sector has passed on news of my return and those on the ground will be expecting me.

Down to 180. I reach forward and pull open my hood, not without difficulty. Immediately, the roar of the slipstream, a blast of cold air and my elbow being buffeted violently. On my downwind leg now and a green light winking at me from below. Eureka! Life on earth!

Down with the wheels — I move the undercarriage lever precisely, forward a fraction, to lift the rotating pins off their stops, then down with a slow but deliberate movement so that it slots into its bottom notch. The aircraft gives the briefest of shimmies as the wheels fall away, there are endless seconds of anticipation, then the slightest of

'clumps', the legs lock into position and the single green light glows on the left of the dashboard.

Curving in now on finals — I push the airscrew into fully fine and feel and hear the engine note rise as the propeller bites. The line of glimlamps stretching away obliquely to my left, flattens out. After which — *flaps*! I flick down the flat disc which operates the flaps and feel the aircraft wallow as they extend — all or nothing at all on a Spit!

Now it's 130, about, and reducing. The airfield boundary coming up at me unseen in the darkness. A final confirmatory green light from the duty pilot at the end of the runway and suddenly the Chance floodlight comes on, bathing the first 100yd of tarmac in a pool of ghostly grey.

Down to 100 and beginning to check, still curving and banking in order to see ahead. My nose well up — high, even. A touch of throttle and a brief surging thrust of engine. Then, holding off. The first flare and floodlight flash past on my left, my nose rising steeply. UP! UP! Small lights stream past. Holding! Holding! Then a *touch*! The Spit balloons minutely before touching again and moving waywardly to one side. I correct — vigorously! Straight — *straight*! I kick hard again to prevent the nose wandering, shouting at the wayward brute. The engine bubbles meanwhile as we surge ahead, unseen gobs of blue exhaust smoke whipping into my face and stinging my eyes. Then everything quietening down. Lights still racing past but slowing. Slower still. A little brake — judiciously — air hissing in spurts from the now maddened cobras beneath my feet. Until I stop. Quivering.

A sigh. I open up and turn towards the intersection I know is there but cannot see. The engine responds gratefully with a comfortable roar, glad to be back on the ground again. I open the radiator and check the temperature. Mustn't let the blighter boil!

Minutes later I follow a tiny nodding torch-beam and brake to a stop. I sense the chocks being placed in position and run the engine gently to get everything circulating. Then, the slow-running cut-out. In the darkness ahead, the noise dies away and the airscrew totters to a clanking standstill. After which there is only darkness. And silence. Broken only by the tick-tick-tick of the exhaust stubs as they begin to cool.

———————

All that was in November 1942 — the last operational flight at night I was ever to make in a Spitfire. Indeed, to the best of my knowledge, the Spit was never again used in the night-fighting role.

The Wartime Fighter Squadron

No 41 Squadron was typical of almost all units then in Fighter Command. Completely self-contained, it was capable of moving around the country and operating independently from wherever it landed. The pilots travelled about in the Spitfires, needless to say; advance party groundcrew by air in such lumbering beasts as Bristol Bombays or Handley Page Harrows, and the main body of airmen usually by motor transport, of which the unit held a considerable amount.

The squadron as a whole consisted of around 200 personnel of all ranks, about 24 of them pilots, of whom more than half were officers and the rest senior NCOs. Single-engined fighter units were then commanded by officers of squadron leader rank (those with twin-engined Beaufighters or Mosquitos had wing commanders in command) and there were on each squadron an adjutant, intelligence officer, engineer officer and doctor, all of them non-flying, older and more mature officers.

The aircraft strength was 18 Spitfires — 16 Unit Establishment, two Immediate Reserve — these being organised into two flights, 'A' and 'B', each under the command of a flight lieutenant, who could be as young as 21. Normally, the squadron was expected to fly a maximum of 12 aircraft, the rest being either unserviceable, under repair, or on inspections of one sort or another.

The squadron commander and flight commanders invariably had aircraft they called their own and which they guarded jealously, but in practice all aircraft were available for use by any member of the squadron.

Pilot Age and Experience

When I was appointed to command 41, I had just celebrated my 22nd birthday. I had flown a total of 655hr of which 395 were 'operational' — the term describing hours flown against the enemy — and despite not having been near a Spitfire for two years, I was expected immediately to lead my squadron

Left:
January 1940: Spitfire Mk Is of No 611 Squadron 'muckin' abaht'. *Flight*

Right:
Pilots of No 41 Squadron operating from Hornchurch during the Battle of Britain when they flew Spitfire Mk Is and IIs. The Squadron Commander, Sqn Ldr D. O. Finlay, is in the centre; Flt Lt Norman Ryder, second from left; and Ft Lt 'Tony' Lovell in the cockpit. Finlay and Ryder — the latter a prisoner of war — survived the war but Lovell was tragically killed in 1945 flying an ex-No 41 Squadron Spitfire XII. Note the old-style Mae Wests and the original black calf-leather flying boots — much treasured. Note also, that almost all are wearing their uniform tunics and slacks — no overalls in those days, unless you bought your own!

into battle, a fairly drastic arrangement which was much less fraught than it would appear.

At the time, the average age of all other pilots in No 41 Squadron was also 22, their individual flying experience ranging from 300 to 600hr. By 1942, all had been through Operational Training Unit (OTU), which would not have been the case early in 1940, when newcomers such as I went straight into an operational squadron having never flown a low-wing monoplane, far less a Spitfire.

Other than those prewar officers and NCOs who had survived, in 1942 pilots throughout Fighter Command were seldom skilled in pure flying techniques, mainly because there was little time for practice flying but also because the aircraft could not be spared from their operational duties unless the squadron was located in some remote area.

Apart from his general lack of flying experience, the average squadron pilot only occasionally achieved more than 25hr flying per month, almost all of which was devoted to operational duties. With luck and good management, he was able to devote one hour per month to shooting against a towed drogue or ground target and perhaps one or two

Right:
The author as a young pilot officer ....

Above:
Stevens and Mungo-Park of No 74 Squadron pose for the camera. The aircraft is a Spitfire Mk I, the gunsight sunscreen having been raised. Stevens is wearing an old-type Mae West with the yellow dope flaking badly and also a pair of non-standard goggles — probably German — the rubber of which would have melted immediately and grafted itself on to his face in the event of a fire in the cockpit. Stevens survived the war but Mungo-Park was killed not long after this photograph was taken. *Flight*

more to practice interceptions, battle formations and fighter attacks. Spinning the Spitfire was generally forbidden and aerobatics regarded as superfluous, although a few exhibitionist loops and rolls over the airfield were tolerated from time to time. Few pilots stalled their aircraft, except by accident or in combat, or had the opportunity to fly on instruments unless in the Link Trainer (Ground Instrument Flying Trainer) or in the course of their day-to-day operational sorties. In short, in most Spitfire squadrons, pilots led a fairly circumscribed life in terms of flying, their shortcomings only revealed when they were later obliged to attend one of the specialist schools of flying or gunnery.

Wings and Stations

On operational stations such as Tangmere, Biggin Hill or North Weald, where there were more than one fighter squadron, the unit became part of a wing, usually of two squadrons, sometimes three. Even so, and despite the wing being led in the air by an officer of wing commander rank, each squadron operated independently in all matters of training, organisation and administration, only becoming part of the wing for major operational sorties.

When based on such stations, the 'maintenance' element of each squadron, as distinct from the first-line section — ie the airmen who refuelled the aircraft and looked after their day-to-day requirements — would move across to become part of the station maintenance section, rejoining the squadron when that unit was transferred on anything other than a temporary detachment.

Right:
One of the several Supermarine S6 series aircraft which won the Schneider Trophy three times in succession between 1929 and 1931 and obtained for Britain the world high-speed record of 407.5mph. The relationship between the S6 and the Spitfire, which flew for the first time five years later, can easily be seen.

With more than 2,000hp 'under the bonnet' and a fixed pitch propeller, landing the S6 was a good deal easier than taking it off, at which time the aircraft demonstrated a powerful urge to dig in and describe a circle in the water. *RAFM P016815*

Below:
The 'R' type 37-litre engine as used in the S6 series aircraft and on which the Rolls-Royce Griffon was eventually based. Termed a 'sprint' engine — its enormous power was only required for a short period — in its final form it was boosted to develop 2,530hp at sea level. Without a conventional radiator, engine temperatures were kept within operating limits by leading the coolant along the sides of the fuselage.

Left:
No description of the Spitfire would be complete without showing the prototype K5054, which first flew in March 1936. Note the fixed pitch propeller, which was changed several times during the initial testing flights before the best performance was obtained, the unique ejector exhausts, and the flat hood. Test pilot Jeffrey Quill reported that it was possible to open the hood in the air at around 300mph, a speed greatly in excess of the maximum of 180 at which later hoods were barely moveable. Unlike the Hawker Hurricane, the Spitfire seldom flew with the hood open except during take-off and landing.

K5054 is pictured here on an early engine run at Brooklands in 1936. On all such occasions the tail had to be held down as the Spitfire would tip up given the slightest encouragement.

Below left:
A beautiful study of the prototype against a cloud background. *Flight 126875*

Above right:
Spitfire Mk I assembly line at the Eastleigh factory in January 1939. *Flight 16698*

Right:
An early Spitfire, P9460 — all curves and beauty.
Rolls-Royce WOP2057

Above:
A brave line-up of the first Spitfires to be used by a
Service squadron in 1938: No 19 Squadron at RAF
Duxford. Note the Watts fixed pitch 'plank' propellers,
the unarmoured windscreens, the ring-and-bead sights,
the original type hood on the second aircraft, and the
protruding outer machine guns, all of which were
changed on later aircraft. No 19 Squadron was
identified by the marking 'QV' during the Battle of
Britain and after.

Left:
A much-used Spitfire Mk I of No 602 Squadron. Note the early type, flat-sided hood with the knock-out panel, the kidney exhaust stubs, and the fabric aileron with the trimming cord stuck on the trailing edge. The propeller is of the metal-bladed de Havilland 20° two-pitch type and the painted diamond on the wing would change colour in the presence of gas. *Flight 17755*

Below:
The same aircraft from the front showing the early black and white under-surface paint scheme. *Flight 17753*

Right:
Armourers' conversation piece: 'There's a mouse down there, I'm pretty sure!' *Flight 17754*

Below right:
The underside of a Spitfire Mk I showing the gun panels and pitot head.
Imperial War Museum (IWM) CH 1-458

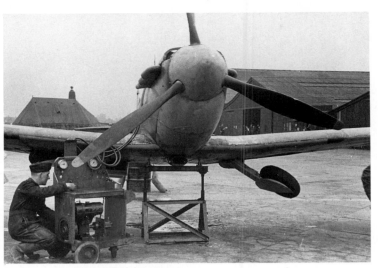

Left:
A rather tired Spitfire Mk I has its undercarriage tested using an external hydraulic source. *Flight*

Centre left:
Don Finlay, one time CO of No 41 Squadron, was an international hurdler who had represented Great Britain in the 1936 Olympics. Finlay commanded the Air Fighting Development Unit at Duxford in 1943 and introduced me to my first Spitfire Mk XII.

Bottom:
The high-speed Spitfire of 1938-39. In an attempt to create a new land speed record, a specially boosted and prepared Merlin 2 was installed in a modified Spitfire Mk 1 airframe and flown at 408mph at sea level. Here, the aircraft is seen with a four-bladed fixed-pitch propeller and an enlarged radiator to cope with the power and heat generated by the engine operating at around 28lb boost and 3,200revs. *Flight 179465*

Top right:
Various Mk I airframes were modified to carry more powerful Merlin engines. This one incorporated a Merlin 20 engine with a two-speed supercharger, a combination which never saw Service use.

Right:
This Battle of Britain Memorial Flight Spitfire Mk I is something of a cheat! The streamlined windscreen, ejector exhausts, and four-bladed airscrew were never seen on original Mk Is. *Jeff Ball*

By the autumn of 1942, the Spitfire Mk Vb had been in service for about 12 months. Understandably, the squadrons closest to the Channel — and the enemy — received the best aircraft and would continue to do so until the Mk V was gradually phased out in Britain during the latter part of 1943. Those squadrons not in the front-line received the less good aircraft, ie, those which were older, those having had a major inspection and with reconditioned engines, or those the frontline squadrons wished to get rid of. Although the distribution of aircraft was always in the hands of 'higher authority', it was a poor squadron commander who did not see to it that his least good aircraft were passed on to someone else. Moreover, it was generally accepted that any Spitfire that had come, secondhand, from one of the Polish or other Allied fighter squadrons, was fit only for the knacker's yard. The Spit in which I had the engine failure within a day of my arrival being one such aircraft, I was in a good position to judge!

Life Span

Fighter aircraft of the time, the Spitfire included, had a life span of 240hr, at which point the aircraft was withdrawn from service and given a major inspection at one of the several Maintenance Units (MUs); 240hr equated to about nine months of flying in the average squadron, although in the main

combat areas not many Spitfires enjoyed a life of even 100hr. Whilst it would be wrong even to suggest that the Spitfire was not built to last, the expectation was that the average aircraft would be lost or heavily damaged, either as the result of an accident or in combat, long before its planned life was completed. This was undoubtedly a factor taken into account during the manufacture of the aircraft and its subsequent deployment; moreover, the technology of the time, together with wartime shortages, imposed restrictions on the use of some materials, resulting in the employment, for example, of magnesium alloy rivets which crystallised with age and tended to lose their heads. Whilst perfectly acceptable in the short term, this proved to be a problem in later years when it was found necessary to replace pretty well every rivet in any refurbished Spitfire.

Inspections

Within the planned lifespan of 240hr, each aircraft was inspected regularly at 30 or 40hr intervals, on which occasions it would disappear into the maintenance hangar and remain there for several days. At the same time, modifications considered to be urgent were carried out, although in the main these were completed when the aircraft underwent its major inspection. During these minor inspections, a prudent pilot timed his leave to coincide

with his aircraft being absent, thus ensuring that some other pilot would not fly his mount and either lose it in combat or damage it — the sentimental attachment between some pilots and their aircraft was sometimes taken to extremes.

And last but certainly not least, there were the DIs, or Daily Inspections. Every aircraft was DI'ed before it could be flown, each tradesman signing the Form 700 for his particular part of the Spitfire, be it instruments, radio, engine, or other, the whole line of signatures being countersigned by the NCO in charge and finally by the pilot when he accepted his mount as serviceable. Later, on completion of his

Above:
Plan view of a Spitfire Mk V fitted with a 'B' wing. There were three wings fitted to a Spit: the Mk Is and most IIs had the 'A' wing and most of the Mk Vs the 'B'. The universal wing, referred to as 'C', was employed on later Mk Vs and all other Merlin-engined Spits, incorporating various permutations of armament.

Left:
Some early Mk Vs of No 72 Squadron besport themselves.

flight, the pilot was obliged to sign the 700 with details of any unserviceability he had encountered or complaints he wished to make. This very important document was the log-book of the aircraft with details and timings of every flight, every fault, and every repair and modification precisely recorded. In deserts, jungles and other faraway places of Empire, wherever there was an RAF aircraft, there was a Form 700 being religiously completed; in fact, in six years of war, I can only recall one occasion during the seige in Malta when 700s were dispensed with in a final desperate attempt to put defending fighters into the air. Woe betide any pilot who even *attempted* to fly an aircraft without first scanning the Form 700 then signing it, and doubly-damned was any airman who put his signature in the appropriate space without properly carrying out his inspection. Their 'Airships', who were hardly given to raising an eyebrow when a Spitfire was lost, with or without its pilot, were apt to go into shock and wreak terrible vengeance if the Form 700 or Authorisation Book were in any way fudged or incomplete.

The Merlin Engine

The Rolls-Royce Merlin engine, with which the Mk V and indeed most of the earlier Spitfires were equipped, was a triumph of mechanical engineering, whose performance was increased to such a degree that, by the end of 1944, the original 1,030hp of the

Merlin 3 — used before and during the Battle of Britain — had been increased in an adapted Merlin 66 to something over 2,000.

Broadly speaking, this increase in power was achieved by modifying the supercharging arrangements, making some internal adjustments and changes enabling greater boost pressures to be employed, and using more advanced fuels, the more sophisticated petrols having the effect of controlling the extremely high temperatures produced in generating the additional 'urge'. By comparison with the Merlin, for the same power output, German engines were of much larger capacity (the Merlin was of 27 litres capacity, the Daimler-Benz 601 of the Bf109, 39 litres, and the BMW 801 of the FW190, 42 litres), a factor which resulted in the Bf109 and the FW190 tending to cruise at higher speeds than the Spit, which they were able to achieve at lower revs and boost settings.

Rolls-Royce's development expertise was, however, entirely lost on the majority of young pilots flying Spitfires, to most of whom the engine was merely a black lump up front; all they were

Below:
The Spitfire Mk V employed any one of about eight different engines, all of the Merlin 45/46 series. This is a Merlin 45. The 'clanking' reduction gear is in the front, the supercharger at the back, the generator and drive in the middle/centre, and the twin magnetos, left and right of the engine, are labelled H.A.

concerned with was that it should keep going, particularly over such sensitive areas as enemy territory and the English Channel, provide the necessary power and respond instantly to the throttle in combat, and not make too much of a fuss in between times.

Superchargers and Boost

In layman's language, the supercharger on the earlier Merlin engines consisted of a single fan, about 9in in diameter, which was driven off the rear of the crankshaft through a set of gears at around 10 times engine speed; if the engine was operating at maximum revs, ie 3,000, the supercharger was turning at 30,000 revs — not exactly dawdling in any man's language! This fan set up a positive pressure in the induction system — referred to as 'boost' — which in British aircraft was measured in lb/sq in, normal atmospheric pressure of just under 15lb being regarded as the datum point and christened '0', the engine then operating at PLUS or MINUS a given number of lb boost. To complicate matters, the Germans measured boost in 'atmospheres' and the

Below:
A Rotol-airscrewed Mk V with blown gun ports being inspected by HM King George VI accompanied by the then C-in-C Fighter Command, AM Sir W. Sholto Douglas. Note that there are at least eight airmen working busily on one aircraft. It never happened to me, alas! *Flight*

Americans in inches of mercury, 30in of mercury being the datum point and each lb of boost approximating to 2in of mercury — thus, 18lb boost became 66in of mercury.

One further and triflingly quaint variation in the use of terminology: whilst we British simply 'flew' at a given boost, the Americans always 'pulled' so many inches of mercury, prompting the more light-hearted of us in the RAF to speculate as to what might have happened had they 'pushed'!

The main purpose of the supercharger was to maintain maximum permitted engine power up to some predetermined height — in the early Spits about 18,000ft. Below that altitude, the supercharger, or blower, to give it its more usual name, provided some welcome additional 'urge', but in order that the engine should not be overtaxed, the extra boost was restricted by a barometrically-controlled device which could be overridden in times of emergency. On the Spitfire this involved pressing a small thumb lever on the throttle quadrant, an operation referred to indelicately as 'pressing the tit'. When this device was activated, the pilot had available to him most of the power the engine was capable of producing, which on the early Spits was 12lb boost. Later 16 and 18lb boost pressures were permitted, and eventually in 1944, with special fuel, plugs, et al, 25lb, at which setting the Merlin engine was generating more than 2,000hp and, in a Mk IXb, nearly hopping out of its frame!

Above:
A posed photograph of a Mk V starting up. It must be posed as the airmen are grinning. Also, there are no wheel chocks! *RAFM P016656*

As it was absolutely necessary that the engine should not be allowed to detonate — 'pink' — supercharger and internal engine development went hand in hand with the production of aviation fuels containing cooling agents such as tetraethyl lead, now the subject of much environmental concern. Other methods involved such simple ploys as injecting water, mostly with methanol additives, into the air-fuel mixture. Both the Germans and the Americans used water injection, the Daimler Benz engines on the later Bf109s and the big Pratt & Whitneys on the American P-47 Thunderbolt being two such examples.

In the early summer of 1940, our Spitfire Mk Is used 87 octane fuel which was considerably less 'pokey' than the two-star or unleaded petrols we use in our cars today. With the result, if we were obliged to 'press the tit' and use the emergency power of 12lb boost, a note of it had to be made in the Form 700 and some sort of convincing explanation given, as it was then necessary to inspect the engine for damage and check the oil filters for traces of

Right:
Myself in EB-V, the No 41 Squadron Spitfire in which I had an engine problem on my first flight. Note that the camera gun in the port wing-root had been pasted over — why, I cannot recall.

bearing. By the time of the Battle of Britain, however, 100 octane fuel was widely available and the use of emergency power became commonplace; indeed, during that four-month period, some pilots 'pressed the tit' on take-off and left it there for the entire flight.

Between 1941 and 1943, a Spitfire Mk V could be equipped with any one of about seven different engines of the Merlin 45 series; however, at squadron level no one paid much attention as to which engine was installed, provided it worked!

Each of the 45-family of engines had a single-stage, single-speed supercharger, designed primarily to improve on the Spit Mk Is performance at 18,000ft by around 20mph and increase its operational ceiling by 1,000 or more feet. All this it succeeded in doing although the difference was only obvious when the engine was run either flat out or at high boost pressures and revs. On normal day-to-day flights at reduced power, the Mk V was if anything marginally slower than the Mk I as it weighed about 600lb heavier.

The use of the engine at high boost pressures and revs became something of a point of contention in 1942-43 as, following complaints from the squadrons that their Spits were being outperformed by the opposition, the manufacturers and the home-based test establishments alleged — with some justification — that the engines were not being used to best advantage, ie at high enough boost and revs. Which was all very well for *them*; they did their high performance testing either on test-beds or over the quiet counties of England, whereas most squadron members spent most of their time 50 miles into enemy territory when there was a natural reluctance to 'cane' their engines except in moments of crisis.

For those of us raised on Spitfire Mk Is and accustomed to seeing 4-6lb on the boost gauge, it came as something of a shock to the system to operate the same engine at anything up to 16lb boost — with all the extra shaking and trembling involved — which was the maximum allowed on all but the later 'cropped blower' Mk Vs.

'Clipped, Cropped and Clapped!'

With the advent of the FW190 in late 1941, it soon became obvious that our Mk Vs were outclassed in terms of performance and urgent steps were taken to remedy the situation, one of which was to produce a Mk V variant with clipped wings and an engine with a cut-down supercharger and boosted to 18lb. This aircraft, designed to give its best performance at 6,000ft and below in expectation of close support duties during the forthcoming invasion, was largely

Right:
A large number of Spitfire Mk Vs were flown by the Americans, both at home and abroad. *Flight*

misemployed throughout 1943, being often used in conjunction with our medium bombers at altitudes up to 20,000ft, at which height its performance had fallen away so dramatically that it was generally inferior to even the ordinary Spit V.

Although very nippy and pleasant to fly low down, the clipped wing Vs were invariably fitted with modified second and third-life engines, whose reliability was uncertain at best, the type as a whole being referred to scathingly as 'clipped, cropped and clapped'.

By the end of the year, the clipped wing Mk Vs had faded from sight — to the relief of scores of pilots who had been obliged to fly them reluctantly for months on end over Europe and the inhospitable waters of the Channel, on tasks for which they were neither intended nor fitted.

Engine Reliability

Engine reliability was, as may be imagined, an important factor in war and my experience was that for its initial life of 240hr, a new Rolls-Royce Merlin could be trusted absolutely, although there were some exceptions, one being if it was in a 'secondhand' aircraft formerly used by some

distinguished but heavy-handed ally. The other proviso was that it had been properly looked after and was not in an area of dust and desert.

Having completed its first 240hr, an engine would be withdrawn, reconditioned at some 'shadow factory', and reissued in another Spitfire airframe. Most were perfectly sound and wholly acceptable but it is more than coincidence that such engine failures as we suffered in No 41 Squadron were almost entirely on reconditioned or second-life engines, the most frequent cause being coolant leaks, both internal and external, leading to overheating and seizure. In addition, there were constant difficulties with engine ancillaries, particularly generator drives, which had a tendency to shear, depriving the aircraft of electrical power and, after a short time, its radio and other vital items, although, I am bound to add, this was more of a nuisance than a fault resulting in casualties.

It was also about this time that there were examples of the Merlin 45 conking out completely when the skew-drive to the magneto stripped, causing the timing of the engine to be totally disrupted — a not infrequent happening, it later transpired, and a very upsetting thing to occur if one happened to be at tree-top height at the time!

Unfortunately, in the turmoil of war, if an aircraft was lost for some obscure mechanical reason, the remains of it were usually swept up and spirited away to some local maintenance unit or to the manufacturer for a post-mortem, after which it was seldom thought necessary to inform those most concerned as to the cause — the squadron which had lost it, and usually its pilot!

When in an operational squadron, I always avoided reconditioned engines whenever I could; to me, shadow factories smacked of backyard garages in Birmingham which, of course, was anything but true. In fact, by far the nicest and most reliable Spitfire I ever flew during the war was an old Mk II of No 53 OTU — with a reconditioned engine!

Finally, the Merlins of Mk Vs operating in Malta and the Middle East were subjected to conditions quite alien to those experienced in England, principally those of high ground temperatures and of dust and sand invading the engine, mostly via the air intake which was situated between the undercarriage legs and within a yard of the ground. This problem caused endless trouble in desert and semi-desert areas, I myself experiencing five engine failures in eight weeks in Malta, admittedly on Hurricanes, but on Merlin engines that were almost brand-new.

Spitfire Mk Vcs sent to Malta in the spring of 1942, were of the tropicalised variety, but the installation of the bulky Vokes filter, which reduced the aircraft's high speed performance by more than 20mph, though of considerable help, was never an entirely satisfactory arrangement.

Below:
January 1942: a tropicalised Mk V, with a Vokes filter up front and a 90gal drop-tank slung beneath.

Above:
This better-looked-after Mk Vb is pictured at Kabrit in Egypt, December 1942. *Howard Levy*

Right:
A tropicalised Mk Vb (or c) wearing No 253 Squadron markings, somewhere 'hot'. Note the neglected state of the aircraft and the airman wearing clod-hopper boots. No high-speed finish on this aircraft!
RAFM P9488

Left:
Gerbini, Sicily — August 1943: a South African Air Force Mk Vb with a revamped filter over the air intake.
Howard Levy

Below left:
Australian Mk Vcs photographed in the Western Desert, and modified to carry bombs.

Revs, Fuel and Mixture

Take-off revs on the Merlin engine employing a constant-speed propeller were 3,000 and the lowest used for general flying, about 1,800. As in a car, low revs were important if fuel was to be conserved — the higher the revs, the more 'essence' down the tube! In combat, conventional wisdom had it that 2,850 was the best setting, otherwise anything from 2,000 to 2,650 was considered appropriate, depending on how much throttle was being used and the various vibration points — whatever the benefits, no one chose to fly at settings at which the engine sounded and felt like a bag of nails! In general, the wider the throttle opening the higher the revs, with high revs being essential above 25,000ft if

any sort of performance was to be maintained. During my first height climbs in a Spit, I could never understand how it was that my flight commander always managed to leave me standing at altitude, until he explained that he habitually went into fine pitch — 3,000 revs — whereas I, with the old two-pitch propeller, would be in coarse and whacking about at around 2,100.

By 1942, the old two-pitch propellers of the earlier Spits had long since given way to the constant-speed variety, on which the pilot set the revs he required and, thereafter, the constant speed unit sorted things out for itself. This comparatively complicated arrangement of high-pressure oil and balances within the spinner of the airscrew was taken very much for granted, one's only awareness of the magic goings-on there being when it threw a film of brown goo all over the windscreen from a seal behind the propeller, appropriately called a Git's seal. For some reason, the Hurricane was especially prone to leaks from the rear of the propeller so that a rim was eventually fitted, not so much to prevent the leaks as to stop the oil from soiling the windscreeen and limiting the pilot's view and his ability to sight his

Left:
The front end of the Shuttleworth Spit which is fitted with a de Havilland metal airscrew and shows the oil tank — a little under 6gal capacity — and the coolant pipe running down to the radiator beneath the wing. This aircraft has the correct exhaust stubs and the camera-gun 'hole' can be seen in the port wing root.

guns. A few Spits, too, had the rim fitted, but it was the exception rather than the rule.

On the earlier Mk Vs, the pilot had the means of selecting weak mixture when operating at low revs and boost, although this facility was seldom used either in day-to-day flying or in combat — it was a very odd chap indeed who chose to roam about over enemy territory with his engine operating at its most economical setting! Except on navigation or reinforcement flights, it invariably became necessary to use the engine at wide throttle openings and, as 4lb boost was the maximum that could be tolerated in weak mixture, pilot-operated mixture controls were eventually considered superfluous and removed from the cockpit.

On flights of long duration, emphasis quite naturally focused on fuel economy as even when full to overflowing the capacity of the Spitfire was a mere 85gal, this being contained in two tanks which sat one upon the other directly in front of the pilot. In 1942, when the Mk V was still regarded as a day-and-night interceptor, this was sufficient for a full-blooded climb and patrol lasting up to about an hour-and-a-half, two hours being squeezed out of the aircraft at a very firm pinch. However, when Fighter Command went over to the offensive in 1941, requiring our aircraft to operate well into continental Europe, it became necessary to carry long-range tanks, the most usual of 30gal capacity and termed a slipper-tank, being hung between the undercarriage legs and held so close to the fuselage that it appeared part of the aircraft itself. Inevitably, it reduced speed by some 10mph but a pilot hardly noticed the difference unless he was required to put his aircraft to the test.

Such tanks gave a much-needed extra half-hour to the endurance and could be jettisoned at will — and mostly were — when crossing into France, or wherever. I always had a mental picture of the farmers of France and Belgium blessing us between very tight lips indeed as a hundred or more long-range tanks rained down on them, their animals and their fields, each day throughout the three years prior to the invasion landings in 1944.

Later, and to meet the needs of Spitfires sent abroad, a small internal tank holding just under 30gal was fitted behind the pilot and long-range tanks of up to 170gal were carried between the undercarriage legs, the larger ones naturally reducing performance very considerably and requiring the aircraft to be flown very circumspectly and without harsh manoeuvres.

The Airframe

As were the airframes of most combat aircraft, that of the Spitfire was modified throughout its service career, being strengthened and altered here and there as more powerful engines were installed, more

destructive armament incorporated, and speeds increased. For these reasons, it very often happened that there were aircraft of the same mark and within the same squadron, with different wings, different windscreens, different types of propeller, and — on the Mk Is — different means of raising the undercarriage. All of which sounds pretty fundamental but, in fact, did not present any problems. Indeed, some pilots remained unaware of the less obvious variations; the aircraft looked more or less the same from the outside, the inside didn't matter that much!

Apart from the propellers, of which there were two main types — the de Havilland metal airscrew and the Rotol Jablo-bladed variety — the principal differences among Mk V Spits were the armament and the wings and ailerons, a so-called universal wing being incorporated into later aircraft of the mark.

The universal wing resulted from the need to strengthen and alter the wing to accommodate either two or four 20mm cannons and ammunition, the original wing being designed to house up to eight .303in machine guns. Cannons had, in fact, been installed into the original wings of some Mk Is during the Battle of Britain, but the squadron involved had complained so bitterly that their guns 'wouldn't work', that the aircraft were quickly withdrawn and thereafter sat unused in a storage depot for quite some time.

Universal or other, the Spitfire's wings were secured at the fuselage end of the main spar by seven bolts the thickness of a man's middle finger. In order to bring home to those going through OTU that there were limits to the load a pilot could impose on a Spit, the spar with its bolts were always shown to all course pupils, a Spitfire having its wing removed for the purpose. This procedure seldom produced other than a pregnant silence among onlookers, although I am bound to admit, I never had first-hand knowledge of a Spitfire wing failure in the air, despite a number of such incidents. What did occur occasionally, particularly on the earlier Spits on which the elevator was extremely sensitive, was that the wings would be given a permanent kink as the result of an over-enthusiastic dogfight or pull-out, resulting in the metal skin wrinkling on the top surface. On the whole though, neither I nor anyone else ever worried about the wings coming off or even bending — indeed the pilot tended to 'bend' long before the aircraft!

In No 41 Squadron at the time, none of our Mk Vbs had the universal wing, nor did we have more than a few with metal ailerons, these being incorporated

Right:
The Shuttleworth Trust Spitfire Mk V being refurbished showing the detached wing and the seven bolts which connected the main spar to the fuselage. *Air Portraits*

retrospectively in order to make the aircraft more responsive at high speed.

Ailerons and Their Problems

The ailerons on the Spitfire were of the 'Frise' variety, and throughout much of 1942 were fabric covered. Light and effective below about 280mph, they became progressively heavier at higher speeds and downright unwieldy at the top end of the speed range.

The Frise aileron, a balanced control, was designed to poke its nose into the airflow when the aileron was raised (and the wing lowered), causing an increase in drag on the inside wing of a turn — which was a good thing. Unfortunately, when travelling at very high speeds and in the level-flight position, both ailerons tended to poke their noses into the airflow at the same time — which was not such a good thing — causing lateral control to become markedly affected, and, it was darkly hinted, resulting in some wing failures.

Whatever, the truth of the matter, in the late summer of 1942, there was so much concern about

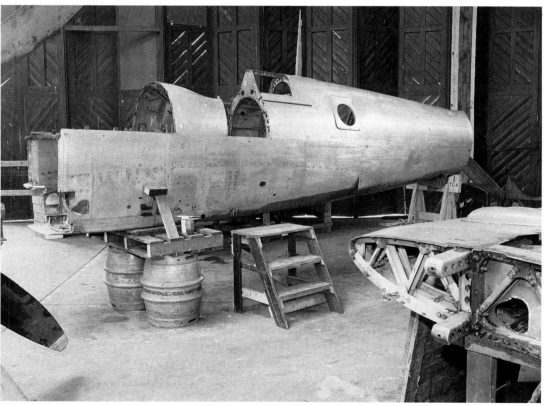

'aileron float' that all our Spitfires had lines painted on the inward ends of their ailerons to enable the pilot to observe from the cockpit whether or not they were rising beyond the danger point. If they showed signs of so doing, a piece of cord was 'doped' on to the trailing edge of each control surface, which had the effect of reducing the float by depressing the aileron — and, of course, making it even heavier to apply!

This 'glueing' of cord to the trailing edge was also employed as a means of correcting any tendency to fly 'one wing low' — and very few Spitfires did not do that! Unhappily, such corrections were not usually effective throughout the entire speed range, so that a pilot had to be satisfied with the best compromise he could achieve by trial and error, the more cord on his ailerons, the heavier the controls becoming.

Even after the introduction of metal ailerons, which lightened the controls very considerably at high speed, there remained the need to correct aileron float and to level up the trim. As sticking on bits of cord was then considered to be passé, I was mildly concerned one day, having asked for my ailerons to be adjusted, to catch my rigger in the act of giving one trailing edge a few hearty wallops with a hide-faced hammer. Assured that up to a point such a remedy was in order, I left him to it, deciding that what the eye didn't see the heart needn't worry about! Sometimes, however, when even a little judicious bashing failed to effect a cure, the ailerons would be removed and swopped around until two were found to be compatible and to operate effectively within the required limits.

This neglect to provide proper aileron trimmers always seemed to me a most irritating oversight, similar to the neglect in putting a rudder bias on the Mk I Hurricane, an omission which caused endless discomfort — if nothing worse — during the Battle of Britain. In fact, this general disregard of trimming devices as well as the neglect of British aircraft designers to provide heat in the cockpits of our fighters, seem now to be almost unforgivable.

The Single Radiator

Because the earlier Spitfires had only a single radiator situated under the starboard wing, apart from its position causing the engine to overheat more quickly on the ground, under most conditions of flight the aircraft tended to fly sideways, if only fractionally. Whilst not troublesome at the lower end of the speed range, it became quite noticeable when going fast, although to some extent it could be counteracted by use of the rudder bias. Even so, on an aircraft on which changes of speed and attitude were many, varied, and very rapid, it was something of a chore being obliged constantly to retrim. Moreover, in the course of a flight during which the pilot's attention was devoted to other more pressing matters — such as not being shot down! — it was seldom that the needles on his turn-and-slip indicator showed his aircraft to be fully in trim, an important consideration when firing the guns.

Windscreens

Also about this time, the earlier arrangement whereby a thick pane of bullet-proof glass had apparently been 'stuck' on to the front of the Spitfire's windscreen, was superseded by a much more sensible affair in which the bullet-proof appendage was properly contained in a streamlined housing which included side panels of reinforced glass which not only could deflect an incoming bullet but allowed the pilot a view not distorted by pieces of curved Perspex. Again, in 1942, there were only several of these improved windscreens in No 41 Squadron.

In Pursuit of Performance

It was also in 1942, after it had become apparent that the Spitfire Mk Vb, with which most of the squadrons on the Channel coast were equipped, was sadly lacking in performance when pitted against the FW190, that strenuous attempts were made to clean up our aircraft. Reams of information and advice came down from Group on the detrimental effect of poorly maintained leading edges and ill-fitting cowlings, studs and fasteners, all this being accompanied by instuctions to repair, adjust, fill in and polish pretty well everything in sight, filler and paint by the gallon being specially provided for the task.

Although we set-to with a will, most of us were privately of the opinion that only the appearance of our aircraft was likely to be enhanced — which turned out to be the case. The walkways and engine cowlings of our Spits, together with access and inspection panels and other vital parts, being tramped on, removed and replaced every day, little could be done to prevent them being 'airmanised',

the average British 'erk' being a specialist in reducing even the most streamlined of forms to something resembling scrap within a month.

The result was, for a period of several months, every cowling on every Spitfire was beaten out, every fastener adjusted, every leading-edge crack and blemish stopped with literally pounds of filler, and every spinner removed, resprayed, then polished to a mirror-like finish. Sad to relate, little improvement in the performance of our Spitfires was discernible; indeed, with all the extra weight of filler and paint, it is probable that they were less spritely than before!

A Voyage Round the Cockpit

To most pilots, the Spitfire appeared a small aircraft, being almost the only fighter low enough to be stepped into, unlike the Hurricane, Typhoon, Mustang and others, into which they were obliged to climb. Quite apart from being easier to get at, the Spit cockpit had a hinged, fold-down flap (to which was attached a crowbar, an implement retained throughout the war and, as far as I am aware, never

used by anyone!) enabling an injured pilot to be evacuated with comparative ease. In a Hurricane, for example, unless the undercarriage was retracted, it was extremely difficult to extract any pilot incapacitated by wounds, it sometimes being necessary to hook the unfortunate man out by crane.

Unlike that of the Hurricane, in which the pilot had the feeling of being suspended in space, the Spit cockpit appeared more cosily enclosed and, by the standards of the time, quite well finished, although there were sharp corners everywhere which took their constant gory toll of ungloved hands.

Though seeming to be confined, it was big enough for even a tall person — I am 6ft 3in — the occupant being immediately aware that he was pretty low down and lodged firmly in a metal bucket seat which snugly accommodated his parachute and, not quite so snugly, his dinghy pack. Ahead, the nose stretched away the length of a cricket pitch — or so it seemed — and in the middle distance and on either side the pilot could glimpse the three rust-brown, kidney-shaped exhaust stubs, the kind then fitted to

Left:
View forward from a present day Spitfire with the nose stretching away 'the length of a cricket pitch'. Here the gunsight has been removed and there would not have been a four-bladed airscrew on a Mk V.

Below left:
The packed dinghy which was attached to the pilot's parachute and on which he sat — not at all comfortably! The lead was hooked on to his Mae West so that the dinghy would not float away in the water.

Top right:
The 'office' of a Mk V, showing the Mk II gunsight — the humane killer — the spade grip control column with the three-way gun button, and the compass low down behind the control column. This aircraft has the later type of flush windscreen.

effective than the hydraulic types. On the other hand, had the Spitfire had more powerful brakes, it would have spent most of its life on its nose as it would tip up given the slightest encouragement.

Having settled himself on his dinghy pack as comfortably as possible — which was not easy! — attached the dinghy to his Mae West (life-saving jacket) by a lead and adjusted the height of his seat, the pilot strapped himself in using his Sutton harness. There were four straps to the Sutton harness — left shoulder, right leg, right shoulder, left leg — which were secured in the area of his tummy by an outsize peg which went through a hole

Below:
Looking tailwards: note the 'blown' hood, the open radio compartment, and the triangle of armour-plate behind the pilot's headrest.

Bottom:
The pilot's bucket seat into which his parachute and dinghy fitted. The so-called 'chassis' is the undercarriage quadrant and lever.

the Spit. This long nose, besides making deflection shooting difficult in combat, was a mildly disconcerting feature to most pilots initially, making taxying something of a problem and being the root cause of many accidents on the ground.

Directly in front was the reflector gunsight, a circle of glass angled in the pilot's direction and attached to a solid metal base on which were circular knurled rings with figures in white. On the part nearest to him was attached a small sorbo pad, there to create the illusion that if his face smacked into it, it would come to no harm — which was the grossest of deceptions, leading to the instrument being referred to occasionally as the 'humane killer'. As one whose face did make contact with the gunsight at least once, I can confirm that it was very hard indeed, sorbo pad notwithstanding!

Immediately ahead at floor level were the rudder pedals with hoops into which the pilot put his feet. Adjustable, they could be screwed in and out and had two tiers, the bottom one being for normal flying and the top to assist him in the event of high acceleration forces being experienced in a steep turn or pull-out — in short, 'g'. Despite flying the Spitfire for years, I never once used the top pedals and I don't know of anyone who did; in fact, unless one consciously moved one's feet beforehand, it was almost impossible to do so once 'g' had been applied.

Linked to the rudder bars were the brakes which were activated by hand using compressed air, so that to press either footrest with the brakes applied was to produce a loud hiss, as though some extremely irritable python had just been kicked into life. Unlike the Germans and Americans, we British always went in for hand-operated compressed air braking systems which, on the whole, were less

and was kept in place by a split pin; the more familiar quick-release box was not available until much later in the war. Inertia straps also being a gadget of the future, he then would flick up his harness release toggle, enabling him to lean forward and adjust his instruments, or whatever. It was important, of course, to return the toggle to the locked position otherwise he was unrestrained in the event of an abrupt stop, in which case the gunsight was usually the first part of the aircraft to remind him of his oversight!

With the pilot in the sitting position and the hood locked open, the controls fell comfortably to hand. Down on his left, the two trimming wheels, the smaller one the rudder bias — forward for right, backward for left — the larger one the elevator — back for up, forward for down, with an indicator on the dashboard to show how things stood. Just behind them, two switches, one for the camera-gun — more of this in a moment — and the second, the pitot-head heater.

The pitot-head was all to do with the airspeed indicator and was situated forward of the aileron under the port wing — the further away from the disturbed airflow, the less the position error. I always considered it vitally important to have the pitot-head heater 'on' for every flight, regardless of the weather and what I was doing; the head itself tended to collect moisture and having it freeze up in cloud meant that the air speed indicator stopped working, which could be very unpleasant. This happened to me twice during the early part of my flying career — once on a dark night — and that occasion particularly taught me a lesson. It was also a wise pilot who remembered not to put his hand on a black-hot pitot-head having finished his flight!

Further forward, then, to the throttle quadrant. By present-day standards, the Spitfire throttle was a puny piece of merchandise but, in comparison with the Hurricane it was positively exotic. The small wooden handle fitted nicely into one's palm and pushing it as far as the 'gate' produced 9lb boost on the Mk V, and through the gate, 12lb. If emergency boost was required, the pilot pushed the thumb switch just forward of the throttle, and eureka! — 16lb (or 18lb on the cropped blower Mk V), although, I have to add, such levels of boost were only obtainable at sea level. During the latter part of 1943, there was a spate of throttle failures on Mk II Spits, which (I was informed) had a suspect hinge at the bottom of the throttle lever which occasionally fractured and left the unfortunate pilot usually with his engine at full bore and a completely detached and useless throttle lever grasped between his fingers!

In the same quadrant was also the mixture control — when fitted — and a lever which controlled the revs, or, more precisely, the engine speed — fine pitch forward, coarse pitch to the rear. There was

also a switch which activated a horn which blew raucously and frightened the pilot almost to death whenever the throttle was fully closed and the wheels still retracted.

It is worth mentioning here that 'engine speed' was not 'airscrew speed', the airscrew being geared down to slightly less than half the speed of the engine through a reduction gear which was familiar to all Spitfire pilots as it 'clanked' very distinctively on start-up and run-down.

Directly above the throttle was the remote control box for the radio, the radio itself, a sizeable piece of equipment, being accommodated several feet behind the pilot and armour plate, usually having the doubtful distinction of being the first vital item to be hit in the event of a successful enemy attack from the rear. The control box was largely similar to the radio in a modern car, with press-button selectors for 'on' and 'off', plus four pre-set frequencies. The control box also had the 'receive/transmit' switch incorporated although this was moved to the control column later in the war. This switch was always spring-loaded to the 'receive' position as, left on 'transmit', no other pilot within a five-mile radius could hear a word being spoken, which, of course, could be critical on an operational sortie. Pilots who left on their transmitters were not popular! — hence the safeguard.

Also on the left-hand side was the lever which controlled the radiator flap — open, closed, and intermediate — a vital piece of equipment, this, as the Merlin engine in the Mk V heated up very quickly on the ground.

The right-hand side of the cockpit was largely taken up with the undercarriage control apparatus, a fairly bulky quadrant labelled 'chassis' with a lever which moved about a foot into the 'up' or 'down' position. There was also a series of buttons and a box darkly referred to as 'IFF' and heavily shielded from prying fingers with a flap and a 'danger' notice, an emergency means of operating the undercarriage incorporating a high pressure CO_2 cylinder, plus the oxygen connection for the pilot — and sundry other knobs and bobs.

Throughout the hundreds of hours I flew in a Spit, I never had an undercarriage failure nor the need to operate the emergency lowering device; the undercarriage may have had its shortcomings but getting it up or down was not one of them! The siting of the quadrant, however, was less good as the pilot was obliged to leave the throttle immediately after take-off, transfer his left hand to the control column and operate the undercarriage lever with his right. On earlier Spits it was even more of an adventure as, after selection, he was obliged to pump up the wheels using a long lever, which usually resulted in his aircraft porpoising around the sky like a frolicking dolphin.

Directly in front of the pilot was the control column, the instrument panel, and underneath the latter, the compass. The control column on the Spitfire Vb was similar to those fitted to all British single-engined fighters throughout the war, in that it had a spade-grip which accommodated the firing buttons for the cannons and machine guns, plus a brake lever which acted in conjunction with the rudder pedals. I never much cared for the spade-grip, much preferring the pistol-grip as used on American aircraft. With the spade-grip I always found myself using two hands when firing the guns which meant that the throttle was left unattended — by no means a desirable state of affairs in combat.

Intending to modify my own aircraft after joining No 41 Squadron, I procured the pistol-grip of an American P-47 Thunderbolt and attempted to make the change, only to find the engineering involved altogether too complicated. Meanwhile, my plan being bruited abroad, I received a furious instruction from 'higher authority' forbidding me absolutely from mutilating items of His Majesty's property. Some years later, all RAF fighters were installed with pistol-grip control columns — which rather proved a point.

The combined three-way gun-button on the control column — with a safety device — enabled the pilot to fire the machine guns and cannons separately, or all together, the 'instruction' being transmitted pneumatically to the guns from the same high pressure air source that worked the brakes, the flaps and the landing lights — when fitted. Run out of high-pressure air, and both fighting and landing became something of a hazard.

The gun-button also activated the camera-gun situated in the wing root — if the camera was working, that is, and if it was loaded, the two seldom occurring at the same time! British camera-guns were miserably indifferent and the recording of aerial combats not taken seriously enough, with the result that the RAF has very little worthwhile to show for the thousands of combat successes it achieved. Although a separate camera-gun button was mounted on the control column, the arrangement whereby the guns and camera-gun were initiated by the same button, resulted in one pupil of No 53 OTU shooting down and killing his own Chief Flying Instructor, who was acting as target in another Spitfire, the pupil believing that he was merely taking a camera-gun picture.

The instrument panel, containing engine, oxygen, fuel contents plus other instruments, buttons, knobs and switches, was dominated by the centrally placed 'blind flying panel'. This consisted of six instruments which were standard on every fighter from the Gloster Gladiator onwards — airspeed indicator, altimeter, artificial horizon, rate of climb and dive, turn and bank indicator, and directional indicator. Later, the Empire Central Flying School insisted on 'blind flying panel' being amended to 'instrument flying panel' and 'turn and bank' to 'turn and slip', neither alteration, I have to reveal, improving my ability to fly the mettlesome Spitfire for long periods in cloud!

Several of the instruments being gyroscopically controlled, every Spitfire pilot was accustomed to seeing his artificial horizon careering crazily from side to side and his directional indicator whizzing across its circle of glass, having toppled his gyros as the result of a hearty turn or some violent manoeuvre, so that it was a prudent fighter pilot who shot into cloud after combat knowing which way was 'up' and which way he was pointing.

The compass on the Spitfire was located behind the control column and between the pilot's knees, a position not altogether satisfactory when night flying or with much of the cockpit in gloom. A little difficult to interpret when moving on to north or south headings, the compass was mainly used to reset the directional indicator — which precessed continuously, of course — but also on its own from time to time, any new course being set on the moveable ring and the aircraft turned until needle and lubber lines were parallel. When very occasionally the compass had a fit of the blues, a bubble would appear, but it very rarely gave trouble and was something of an old faithful. Every now and then it had to be 'swung', the Spitfire being taken to a compass base usually at the far end of the airfield, after which the pilot and one companion would 'skive' for a full morning or afternoon, pushing the aircraft onto the cardinal headings and correcting the errors disclosed with magnets and keys.

The Hood

The hood on the Mk V was little different from that fitted to the Mk I, and unlike that of the Hurricane, had two positions — open and shut! It was always locked in the open position on take-off and landing, otherwise it was kept closed at all other times. In the air, even with brute force, it could not be opened at speeds above 180mph and in order to do so the pilot reached forward and pulled at the toggle catch above his head. In the air, it went forward much more easily than it moved backwards.

The view from the closed hood of a Spit Mk V was only a little better than adequate, the pilot being low down, the nose long, and the vision rearward somewhat restricted. Fortunately, it was much better than that from the Bf109, the hood of which was a brute and had bars everywhere. Much later, the bubble hood of the Mk V was replaced by one of the teardrop variety. Various later marks also had the teardrop hood which permitted an infinitely better all-round view, the rear of the fuselage being redesigned at the same time.

The jettison arrangement on all of the earlier Spits, including the Mk V, was fairly primitive, a

Above left:
The hood, showing the hand-holds and the scent-spray rubber ball which operated the jettison mechanism . . .

Left:
. . . and here are the wire and pins that held the hood in place until it was jettisoned. Bottom left is the tip of the crowbar with which the pilot attacked the hood if it didn't come off.

wire passing from the catch above the pilot's head to a series of nail-like pins which held the base of the canopy in its grooves. Pull the wire by its small scent-spray rubber ball and the pins were tugged out of their holes, allowing the hood to move away from its housing. After that, the pilot exercised leverage with his elbows or hands and the whole thing disappeared astern — he hoped! Not all hoods came off without a struggle, however, the crowbar attached to the side of the cockpit attesting to such difficulties.

Finally, all Spits were fitted with a small rear-view mirror which was situated above the hood. However, as so many Spitfires were shot down from dead astern, one can only conclude that the mirror was placed there mainly for psychological reasons. Personally, I never found it of much use other than to confirm that at least some of my squadron were following me!

Armament and Armour

The prototype Spitfire of 1936 was never designed to accommodate 20mm cannons. It caused some concern, therefore, when it became clear in 1940 that a much heavier calibre weapon than the .303in machine gun was required, a problem compounded by the fact that the only 20mm cannon around — the drum-fed Hispano — was neither reliable nor available in the numbers required.

As already mentioned, the first cannons were fitted into a squadron of Mk I Spitfires during the Battle of Britain with very indifferent results and it was only when further thought and effort were given to housing the 20mm gun more sensibly in a blister built into the top of the Spitfire wing that a severe jamming problem was overcome.

By the summer of 1942, cannon trouble had largely been resolved in the Spitfire Vb, although stoppages were by no means infrequent, and it was not until

Above:
Armourers' conversation piece: 'If you'll press the button, I'll look down this 'ole and see if anything comes out!'

Left:
Armourers load 20mm belt ammunition into a Spitfire fitted with a 'C' wing. Normally each cannon was loaded with 120 rounds which allowed about 12sec of continuous fire. The Browning machine guns, with 300 rounds each, had around 15sec of fire.

Below left:
The cannon magazines in a four-cannon 'C' wing.
RAFM P9165

the stronger and more accommodating universal wing was in production that a final solution was reached. Even so, I was never really comfortable using the cannons in a Spitfire, as they thumped quite violently when fired, the aircraft slewing sideways when, for whatever reason, one of them stopped. I am bound to add, however, that when a target was hit with 20mm shells, the effect was almost frightening, as unlike German cannon ammunition which, because of the lower muzzle velocity of the Oerlikons, usually exploded on impact, our ammunition positively mutilated anything it struck.

In order to keep the cannons and machine guns clean and reduce the risk of freezing at altitude, special lubricants were used, the machine gun ports in the wings covered with patches of doped-on fabric, and the muzzles of the cannons protected with plastic gaiters. These gaiters — which went by many names! — were also used for many purposes, one of which was to make life easier in winter for Perkin, the No 41 Squadron French poodle mascot, who frequently wore four on his paws and one on his tail!

Left:
For me a sad photograph: Perkin, the No 41 Squadron French poodle mascot with four cannon gaiters on his paws and one on his tail, with Rex Poynton, my Flight Commander, who was the first officer of No 41 Squadron to be lost on Spitfire XIIs in April 1943.

Of the four Colt/Browning machine guns in the Mk V, little need be said other than they worked perfectly, their only shortcoming being the size of their projectiles.

Although the Mk V Spit had enormous success against the opposition, it was, in my opinion, by no means the best gun-platform in the world. Moreover, as the view over the nose was limited — even worse on the Mk IXs — deflection shooting was never easy. Which was the reason why most successful attacks were made from within 15° of dead astern, that and the fact that many pilots — British and German — were not only incapable of launching a successful deflection attack but constantly misjudged their ranges, believing 500-600yd to be a mere 200.

At anything less than 150yd range, an enemy aircraft appeared almost to be within touching distance and a rapidly overtaking pursuer ran a grave risk of being hit by flying debris if any substantial strikes were achieved. Few pilots did other than fire both cannons and machine guns together; the opportunities were so fleeting it was pointless being selective. Moreover, although the guns on a Spit were normally synchronised to form a group at 200-250yd range, not many pilots were sufficiently interested to check exactly how the guns were aligned on the aircraft they were flying.

As an adjunct to successful air fighting, the Mk 2 Reflector Sight — otherwise the familiar humane killer — with which all Spitfires were equipped until the gyroscopic sight came into service in late 1944, was only moderately successful in the sense that, although it provided a useful means of correctly assessing the range of all sizes of target aircraft, it was only a little more advanced than the old ring-and-bead sight of World War 1 when it came to deflection shooting. Not only did target size and range have to be pre-set on the serrated wheels below the sight, but experience showed that many pilots ignored the presentations offered — which more than anything, attested to the tensions and excitement of combat flying.

As regards protective armour, a pilot in a Spit was well insulated against attacks from the rear by slabs of plate covering both his back and his head. From

Below:
Extending under the pilot's seat was the main piece of armour-plate in a Spitfire (the headpiece is not shown here). My experience was that it would withstand a bullet or cannon-shell fragment fired at 200yd range or more but could be penetrated by an armour-piercing projectile from closer range.

the front there were the Merlin engine and his bullet-proof windscreen to protect him and the cowling over the fuel tanks was resistant enough to deflect a glancing bullet or shell. The armour-plate itself was incredibly tough — and heavy — weighing several hundred pounds and, being about ¼in thick, could withstand a direct hit from either German machine gun bullets or cannon shells from around 200yd. Fortunately, German cannon shells usually burst on impact with the Spitfire's metal fuselage and their bullets made little more than dimples in the protective plate. From closer range, however, the armour could quite readily be pierced; in fact, I have seen a .5in armour-piercing bullet from an Italian Macchi 202, go straight through two pieces of armour-plate in addition to the pilot!

Other Aspects of Flying

True and Indicated Airspeeds

When the Spitfire first made its appearance in 1936, it was widely described as having a top speed of 362mph. About 16 years of age at the time, I fondly imagined that every Spitfire raced around the sky at six miles per minute, which was far from the truth.

The speeds of all aircraft are quoted as 'true' airspeeds and not the speed seen by the pilot 'on the clock', which is termed 'indicated' airspeed. This, quite simply, is because the airspeed indicator is calibrated to read correctly at ground level, or more precisely at ICAN conditions approximating to ground level. (ICAN = International Congress of Air Navigation; the conditions 15°C and 1013 millibars atmospheric pressure.) More graphically, at every height other than ground level — the only height at which he never flies! — a pilot's airspeed indicator is grossly in error.

As a rule of thumb, and despite there being other small built-in inaccuracies, true airspeed (TAS) is roughly calculated as being indicated airspeed (IAS) plus 3% of IAS every 2,000ft. Thus, with one's instrument registering 250mph at 20,000ft, the aircraft's true airspeed would be approximately 325mph — 250 + (3 × 2.5 × 10).

One further minor point: throughout the war, instruments on RAF fighter aircraft registered mph, whereas nowadays speeds are invariably quoted in nautical mph (or kt), the nautical mile representing one minute of latitude (distance) on the maps normally used by airmen and others.

All Spitfires in the RAF were limited to a diving speed of 450mph indicated, which, achieved at, say, 16,000ft, meant that they were flying at around 560 — no mean speed!

On normal training exercises and flying about at, say, 2 to 4lb boost and 2,400rpm, the Spitfire Mk Vb would clock around 240mph — a far cry from its absolute maximum of 370, a computed speed, which

could only be achieved at the aircraft's 'best height' — about 18,000ft — where a combination of supercharger effectiveness and reduced air density provided the optimum conditions.

Straight and level and at ground level, it was a good Mk V that would achieve much above 295mph indicated, even at 16lb boost, the aircraft not being designed for maximum efficiency low down. It was, moreover, a flight condition that could only be maintained for about 5min, fuel consumption being disproportionately high, the engine meanwhile, operating at high revs and showing every sign of being under stress.

In fact, there were very few occasions when it became necessary to fly 'flat-out' low down and I doubt that any two Spitfires produced exactly the same performance, top speed being more of a statistic of comparison than a major factor in day-to-day operations.

Radio and Control

Prior to the outbreak of World War 2, the RAF was not altogether accustomed to using radio, and Radio Direction Finding, as radar was at first termed, was a highly secret development and then in its most primitive form. Even after the commencement of the Battle of Britain, only those fighters in No 11 Group — the area around London — used VHF radio, the rest being on HF, on which frequencies those of us flying Spitfires in Yorkshire, for example, were just as likely to get the BBC fatstock prices as we were the sector controller giving us information of a German attack on Hull.

By 1942, all fighters had been fitted with VHF radios and radar had improved considerably, although it was still in the dinosaur stage when compared with radar as we know it today. Moreover, Air Traffic Control did not exist, its forerunner being termed Flying Control and consisting of anything from one very bored NCO pilot who alternated between making tea in a so-called Watch Office and operating a green and red Aldis lamp at the end of the airfield, to several controllers working in shifts from a suitably located building on the airfield. There, all air movements were co-ordinated and dealt with, the controllers being additionally responsible for passing on weather information and barometric pressures and providing a simple direction-finding and homing service. Needless to say, there were no such luxuries as Ground Controlled Approach or any sophisticated landing aids, the squadrons and pilots coming and going more or less as they pleased.

Operationally, fighters were controlled by Sector, which could be 50 miles away from the aircraft's base, and carried out on the basis of plots from fairly primitive high and low-looking radars and Observer Corps reports — radar height-finding was still in its infancy and not usually very accurate.

Because of these limited resources, even in 1942-43, a single-seat fighter pilot had to have his wits about him as he was obliged not only to fly his aircraft and fight, but also to navigate himself around the sky, as often as not in miserable weather conditions and, on at least some occasions, find his own way home.

To help him and to enable inter-aircraft communication, he had four pre-set radio channels at his disposal, the selection of which he made by pressing one of four buttons on the remote control in his cockpit: 'A', was always local control, which included the limited homing service; 'B', a Sector frequency on which he was controlled when operational, or if he wished to be controlled on training exercises — sometimes he didn't; 'C', a frequency common to his own and adjacent Sectors and also used for control, fixing, and landing on other airfields; and 'D', the distress frequency, which dealt only with 'Maydays'.

Needless to say, if his radio were damaged in combat or went 'phut', he was on his own, a particularly unnerving experience when operating in bad weather or over blacked-out Britain on a dark night. On the whole, though, by 1942, radios were fairly reliable, although it was sometimes the case that the generator would fail in his Spitfire or not be switched on as the result of an oversight, in which event his only link with the ground would die away to a terrible silence as the battery became exhausted.

As an aid in controlling their charges, Sector frequently made use of IFF (Identification Friend or Foe), the equipment itself being deemed very hush-hush and only spoken of behind guarded lips. Having been invited to 'flash your weapon', the pilot would switch on his IFF, causing his particular radar blip to be identified by a 'feather'. So important and secret was this equipment considered to be that a detonator was fitted in every fighter enabling the IFF apparatus to be blown up were the aircraft to land in enemy territory.

Interestingly enough, the subject of IFF remained part of every operational briefing throughout the war and scores of sets were destroyed by devoted pilots who were forced down in enemy territory and who carried out this duty even to the point of jeopardising their own freedom, although by 1945 the Luftwaffe was thoroughly familiar with the equipment and could probably have filled an aircraft hangar with captured IFF sets. On the Spit Mk V, the IFF apparatus was behind the pilot's head and the detonator switches conveniently located alongside his right hand.

Flying the Mk V at Altitude

Even with a single-stage supercharger, the Spitfire Mk V was quite at home at 30,000ft and could struggle up to more than 37,000ft if the pilot had the time and the inclination to persevere. Much above 30,000ft, however, fighting was difficult and anything like a sustained series of steepish turns could only be undertaken with considerable loss of height. Combat at altitude, in fact, other than long stalking climbs against high-flying reconnaissance aircraft, was usually limited to swoops, curves and thundering dives, with the Spitfire capable of achieving a Mach number of at least .85 — more than the Meteor jet 15 years later! It was, moreover, very cold up there and difficult to breathe. Later, the Mk IXa romped around at up to 42,000ft, where, without pressure or heat in the cockpit, very little — apart from the scenery — was at all pleasant.

At height, the engine had to be used to the maximum — the throttle up to the gate and beyond — in order to squeeze out all that was left of the boost, the revs being advanced to around 2,850. This, plus the comparatively low airspeeds experienced — the best climbing speed was down to 120mph indicated above 30,000ft — and the smaller volume of air passing through the radiator resulted in high coolant temperatures. These sometimes bordered on the maximum of 115°, although paradoxically, the oil had a tendency to freeze in the oil cooler, which was situated under the port wing. If that happened, as the oil would then by-pass the cooler, the oil temperature would soar towards the maximum of 90° and the pressure drop with a thump, an alarming state of affairs when well into enemy territory, as there was no immediate remedy. On such occasions, the pilot was obliged either to sit it out, hoping that the engine would survive the ordeal, or drop down to a lower altitude, trust that the enemy would not take note of his predicament, and pray that the oil in the cooler would unfreeze itself.

Regarding oxygen, as is well known, the air pressure (or density) at 20,000ft is about half that at sea level, and at around 33,000ft, one-fifth, a convenient height to mention as only one-fifth of the air we normally breathe is life-sustaining oxygen. If, therefore, a pilot ventured much above 33,000ft, even breathing pure oxygen, he suffered from oxygen starvation — hence the need either for extra pressure within the cockpit, serving to reduce the effective altitude, or a type of pressure-breathing equipment capable not only of forcing oxygen into his lungs but also of providing some compensating pressure around his chest to prevent him being inflated like a balloon, if only mildly. Moreover, operating in an environment of one-fifth normal air pressure, it was five times more difficult to speak!

Our oxygen system in the Spitfire until about mid-1941, was simple; oxygen compressed into cylinders located behind the pilot, was led through a tap, regulator and indicator on the left-hand side of the dashboard to a rubber tube which was connected to a mask clipped to the pilot's leather helmet. The

mask itself, which also accommodated his radio microphone, was mainly of stiffened fabric and fairly loose fitting, the oxygen being squirted in a constant stream in the general direction of nose and mouth — if the pilot remembered to switch it on, that is! If he did not — and it did happen occasionally in moments of excitement and stress — although he would survive quite comfortably up to about 15,000ft, towards 20,000ft he ran a grave risk of lapsing into unconsciousness. At 25,000ft, without oxygen, it was an unusual pilot who was able to retain his wits about him for more than several minutes, and at 33,000ft and above, not only was he likely to fade away in seconds but, as described, even with full oxygen, he suffered from oxygen starvation.

On the Mk V, the system was a little different as, with our aircraft fulfilling a different role and tending to operate at greater heights for longer periods, it became necessary not only to conserve oxygen but to make sure the pilot was better provided for. Consequently, the loose-fitting fabric mask gave way to a snug-fitting rubber creation which was fed by a much wider flexible tube from an 'economiser', which was part of a so-called demand system — the pilot 'demanded' it when he inhaled. However, there was also an arrangement whereby if, for one reason or another, he didn't demand it, oxygen was then puffed into his face. The oxygen bottles, pilot's controls, indicator, et al, remained the same; the economiser, which looked like the bellows used to invigorate a log-fire, was tucked away beneath the pilot's seat on the right-hand side of the cockpit.

Not only was the proper provision of oxygen vital in keeping the pilot alive, it was also necessary to keep him alert and warm and enable him to see properly, particularly at night. For these reasons, it was the drill on all operational sorties to switch on the oxygen immediately the engine was started. Anoxia was — and remains — an insidious enemy, creeping up on its victims unaware, a pilot's critical faculties the first to be affected. The worse his condition, the better he felt — until, oblivion! Losses through anoxia were fairly regular throughout the war — in the average Spitfire squadron, probably one pilot and aircraft every six months.

Also directly linked to reduced air density at height, was reduced temperature, the pilot's rule-of-thumb calculation being a loss of 2° centigrade (Celcius) per 1,000ft. Thus, at 35,000ft, regardless of ground temperature and conditions, there would be a difference of 70° centigrade — and an ambient temperature of minus 60°, or thereabouts, is a pretty cool environment in which to sit, stay alert, and fight for any length of time, particularly when the Spit V was not equipped with any form of cockpit heating — an almost incomprehensible omission.

In this respect, the Spit, having a much more enclosed cockpit, was by no means as painful to fly in as a Hurricane Mk 2 which had holes in the floor and draughts galore, so that in that aircraft the pilot was rapidly reduced to a semi-crystalline state and soon ceased to care very much about anything.

The Spitfire was, however, equipped with a de-icing system in the event of the cockpit icing or misting up, which it did regularly, having been at height for any sustained period. In any such event, a knock-out panel was provided on the port side of the canopy, allowing the pilot some sort of clear view to one side. This small oval panel at face height, appears in many photographs of wartime Spitfires, giving the occupant the appearance of an Al Jolson 'nigger minstrel'.

As the result of these high altitude problems, a few Mk Vs were built with sealed cockpits and a pump providing several pounds of internal pressure. Reclassified the Mk VI, the aircraft had extended wingtips, the pilot having the cockpit hood screwed down over his head when in dispersal, a slightly alarming procedure, this, as no one with any sense ever took off or landed a Spit with the hood closed, and one's fitter or rigger, unable to pass a final word of encouragement, was apt to bang on the closed hood and pull a face, giving the impression that he never expected to see the man inside again! Even so, the Mk VI was pleasant enough to fly, being much quieter (and warmer!) than the ordinary Mk V, although the controls were stiffer because of the pressure-proof seals around the control cables, and the elevators a little odd because of stability difficulties, although no one took much account of such trifles!

Pilot Aids and Equipment

Although no one paid much attention at the time, in terms of flying clothing, Spitfire pilots in 1942 were not very well provided for. Most still retained — but seldom wore — the old Sidcot flying suit, which was a bulky fur-collared, waterproof affair more suited to the mid-1930s and open cockpits. Each pilot also had a 'goon-skin', a fleece-lined Irvin suit consisting of coat and trousers, some coats having an attached fur-lined hood. Few pilots ever wore the trousers but the coat was in great demand, although not for flying, being altogether too bulky for regular use in a Spitfire cockpit. Moreover, when it was worn occasionally to stave off the misery of winter cold, the jackets with hood attached were a positive menace as, turning quickly to search for the German fighter on his tail, the pilot's face was apt to disappear into the woolly lining of the hood, that part of the garment not turning with his head.

By far the greatest hazard in combat was being burned by fuel fires in and around the cockpit. These developed very quickly and temperatures of several thousands of degrees were generated within seconds, incinerating hands and face in a matter of moments, particularly if the aircraft canopy were opened in preparation for evacuating the aircraft. For this reason, it was very quickly appreciated that it was essential to keep covered the hands, face, and feet, thereby ruling out the shirt-sleeve sorties that were almost de rigueur during the first few weeks of the Battle of Britain.

Despite these painful lessons, the RAF did not provide its pilots with any lightweight, flame-proof flying suit, most pilots going to war in their second-best uniform tunic and slacks or using a linen overall purchased privately. In fact, far from being equipped with a suitable fire-proof garment, there was no overall of any description available until well after the war, fighter pilots in the Middle East even going into combat with bare knees and arms.

However, decent flying boots and gloves were available; the boots were originally of fleece-lined black calf leather, but successive designs degenerated through various stages to something of similar appearance but cheaper materials. Several characteristics, though, they all had in common: they all tended to fly off in the air at the first tug of an opening parachute, and a pilot could not walk in any of them for any distance, an important consideration when there was a possibility of being shot down and then escaping, mostly on foot. For these reasons, a so-called 'escape boot' was later designed, the top of which could be cut off with a knife and made to resemble an ordinary black shoe. Equipped with a lining, it did provide quite reasonable protection from the cold and enabled the pilot to walk at least for a time, if not very comfortably.

The gloves remained the same throughout the war, however: soft cape leather next to the skin, then silk inners, and finally leather elbow-length gauntlets, all three being worn together but even combined, being totally unequal to the ravages of minus 60° centigrade at 34,000ft!

Throughout the war, too, all fighter pilots wore life-jackets, termed 'Mae Wests'. Containing some flotation kapok, the early design was a pale green in colour and had to be daubed yellow with aircraft dope. Not having a CO_2 bottle, it was pretty inefficient and needed to be inflated by mouth 'on the way down' which, if the wearer were wounded, injured or burnt, was asking rather a lot. Moreover, without the means of preventing it rising under the pilot's chin, in a choppy sea it was just as likely to throttle him as preserve his life.

By 1942, however, the Mae West was a far more sophisticated piece of equipment, with automatic inflation, flares, a whistle, a light, and a stain to mark the water, besides being of a naturally yellow material and much more comfortable to wear. There were also ties which prevented it lifting and forcibly drowning him.

By far the greatest aid to a fighter pilot's salvation, however, was his seat-type dinghy, brought into service in the spring of 1941. This was attached to the pilot's parachute and took the place of the sorbo cushion under his behind, being very much an uncomfortable substitute as the quite substantial steel CO_2 bottle made itself painfully obvious. Modified and improved upon throughout the war, the dinghy was clipped on to the pilot's Mae West when he entered the cockpit and accompanied him down to the sea when he used his parachute, being tethered to his person by a lead and unable to float away. However, not all of the early dinghies worked; the first of mine refused to inflate when the CO_2

Below:
A pilot in his dinghy and the most welcome sight in the world — an approaching Walrus. The Walrus crews were the bravest of the brave, often venturing in aircraft that were almost unarmed and highly vulnerable to within yards of the enemy coastline and harbours. *RAFM P1173*

Right:
Dated April 1942, this picture is included to show the pilot who, quite extraordinarily, is sitting on the wing in his parachute and without either a dinghy or a Mae West. However, it does show something of the headgear of the time and how the parachute was attached. *Flight*

bottle 'froze' when activated, after which — only partially blown up — it disappeared beneath the waves in a flurry of bubbles, having by some means sustained a 6in gash in its rubber side.

There were several occasions, too, when the dinghy, uninvited, came to life at altitude in a Spitfire cockpit, requiring the pilot to subdue the hissing, expanding monster which was threatening to fill his entire domain. As the result of these quite alarming incidents, all pilots were issued with a knife to stab the brute to death!

The leather helmet in 1942 was an unremarkable item, which, refined in 1940, virtually remained unaltered for the rest of the war — 'bone-domes' were still some 13 years away and could not have been used anyway in the confined space of a Spitfire cockpit. To it were attached the oxygen mask and microphone, the radio earpieces and a pair of goggles — these considered essential and worn religiously in view of the ever-present fire risk, although not every pilot pulled them down over his eyes during an operational sortie believing them to impair his vision. In fact, they were very good (and have been worn by motor-cyclists ever since!) and, although they tended to mist up occasionally, they could be kept clear with the use of the 'mist-free' ointment provided. The incidence of head injury in fighter aircraft, though considerable, was never regarded by pilots as being a major problem, whereas mortal damage from burns most definitely was.

In an operational Spitfire squadron, the helmet, with attachments, was usually left in the cockpit, hooked over the gunsight or the control column and with the radio lead plugged in, the parachute and dinghy remaining in the bucket seat or draped over the tailplane, according to taste. The parachute was repacked once a month, at which time it was returned to the parachute section and hung out to air. If used — provided the pilot returned and was in a fit state to make the gesture — it was the done thing to tip the parachute packer 10/- (50p), which may sound miserly but not when a pilot officer's salary of 11/10d (60p) per day is taken into account.

In six years of war in fighter aircraft, I never once saw a pilot wearing his helmet outside the cockpit, and the frequently-shown publicity photographs and films of pilots racing for their aircraft clad in their headwear and with parachutes dangling from their rear ends, are too ridiculous for words.

Abandoning a Spitfire

During an operational tour of 200hr in an active combat area — and most fighter pilots did two tours, if they survived — the chances were that a pilot at some time would be obliged to ditch, bale out, or force-land his Spitfire. The decision to bale out was easy enough to make if the aircraft were badly crippled or on fire, much less so if it were merely damaged or had engine trouble, the great temptation then being to remain in the cockpit.

The approved method of baling out was to open the hood, turn the aircraft on its back, undo the straps, and push — at which time the occupant departed like a champagne cork. Mostly, however, such a contrived method was unnecessary as it only needed him to stand up in his open cockpit to be sucked out. In fact, there were as many ways of abandoning a Spitfire as there were pilots who were obliged to do so; any way was good enough in an emergency, the main hazard of an 'over-the-side' method being striking the tailplane or having the parachute caught up in it.

Finally, although the Spitfire force-landed easily and safely enough with wheels retracted, it did not ditch at all well, heading usually for the sea-bed in a trice; the Spit definitely did not float! This was mainly due to the weight distribution and the position of the radiator under the wing which acted as a scoop and tipped its nose down.

Although there were a few successful ditchings, because hitting the sea was largely similar to flying into a brick wall — the result being much the same — the drill was to abandon the aircraft whenever possible and hope to preserve life by the use of parachute, dinghy and Mae West.

Combat

Much has been said and written about the Spitfire in combat and, as opinions vary, I can only give a personal view. My first and most vivid impression of the Spitfire early in 1940 was that whilst it was delightful and exciting to fly — rather like driving a souped-up Bentley around Brand's Hatch without having to pay for the petrol; it was unusually sensitive on the elevators. Push the control column forward with anything more than a touch and you were out of your seat and half-way through the roof; pull back more than was prudent and gravity was dragging you down and everything going black within seconds.

In fact, the fore-and-aft stability of the Spitfire was only marginal throughout its entire life, a shortcoming ameliorated in the short term when bob-weights of varying sizes were attached to the elevator balance, making the elevator more difficult to apply with 'g'.

This, in some ways, admirable combat characteristic of the Spit was almost entirely nullified by the tendency of the Merlin's carburettor to flood after the briefest period of negative 'g'. On such occasions, yards of black smoke would gush from the exhausts, the engine would cease to pull for a second or two, and the Bf109 or FW190, whose

Right:
What a German pilot hoped never to see — a Mk Vb of No 152 Squadron at spitting distance.

direct-injection engines suffered no such ill-effects, would pull away to the extent of several hundred yards. This small interval of time was so vital when chasing an enemy, that it led to Spitfire pilots half-rolling their aircraft in order to keep their engine running in an attempt to minimise the advantage their opponents gained.

Contrary to general belief, there were very few knock-down-drag-out dogfights even in the halcyon fighter-versus-fighter days of 1941-43; most engagements resolved themselves into dives, swoops, soaring climbs and chases, lasting from a few seconds to a minute or two at the most, the majority of those shot down — German and Allied — being victims of attackers they never at any time saw.

German fighter pilots, well aware of the behaviour of the Merlin engine and even more aware of the Bf109's lack of lateral control at high speed, fashioned their tactics accordingly. Being nimble and fast accelerating aircraft, they were adept at diving steeply to attack and either continuing their dive or climbing rapidly away. As such tactics seldom involved them in turning exercises, the main ingredient of the classic dogfight rarely presented itself.

Because of the apparent reluctance of enemy fighters to become embroiled in steep-turning engagements, there was always the comfortable belief among Spitfire pilots that theirs was the more manoeuvrable aircraft, although tests with captured German aircraft proved this to be only marginal other than at very high speeds. The truth was pilots on both sides exploited the best characteristics of their aircraft so that smallish differences in straight-and-level speeds and turning circles did not count for much when weighed against surprise, nimbleness, weapon effectiveness, and the ability to accelerate away in either a dive or a climb.

All things considered, the Spitfire Mk V was fairly even-Stephen with the Bf109F and G, and having seen the enemy in time, the pilot of a Spit could always expect, if not to triumph, to avoid being shot down. With liquid-cooled powerplants, both types of aircraft were highly vulnerable to damage in the cooling system, the engine of each overheating and seizing up within minutes of a strike.

Not so the FW190, which had an air-cooled radial engine initially, of very considerable size and power, and which, greatly superior in speed, could dictate the terms of any engagement, coming and going as it

Above:
When not expecting to be in contact with the enemy, most Spitfire squadrons flew around in formations looking like this. *Flight*

pleased. Only later when the Mk IX and Mk XII Spitfires were introduced in 1943, did things change for the better.

Finally, I am almost reluctant to mention ground attacks against targets of opportunity which, from 1941 onwards, were carried out in scores over France and Belgium by Spitfire squadrons based in

Below:
A Mk Vb of No 501 Squadron which came to grief on the enemy coast. *RAFM P9888*

Above:
Another Mk Vb which crashed in enemy territory, the pilot having neglected, or been unable, to blow up his IFF set — there is no hole behind the pilot's canopy.
RAFM P018066

the southern counties of England. Allegedly to encourage the offensive spirit but also for political reasons, these ridiculous forays resulted in the deaths of countless gallant and experienced pilots who were sacrificed with very little to show for their efforts. The Spit was never designed for, nor well suited to, ground attacks; the view ahead and below was indifferent, with its exposed radiator it was highly vulnerable to ground fire, and its armament was hardly effective against water towers, small buildings, armoured vehicles, or even steam loco-

motives — although to shoot up a steam engine was always satisfying. Later, during the invasion of Europe, the Spitfire was employed to better effect using bombs, but that was a different mark of Spit — and a different story!

Left:

A Mk VI, high altitude fighter, which was little more than a converted Mk V. I flew several belonging to No 124 Squadron in 1943 and found them pleasantly quiet if a little stiff on the controls; however, I did not like being screwed down into the cockpit one little bit. This one has extended wingtips and the small bulge below the exhausts is the air intake to the cockpit compressor, the aircraft having a fairly primitive pressure cabin.

Below left:

The Mk VIII was the 'real' Mk IX, the latter being something of a stop-gap aircraft. I flew a number of Mk VIIIs and, operationally, liked them more than almost any other Spit. This one, with its skirts down whilst landing in Comilla, India, had the smaller rudder of the Mk IX.
Howard Levy

Top right:

A more conventional Mk VIII with the so-called broad chord rudder. In fact, there were several models of Mk VIII — for high, low and medium altitude operations — with different 60 series engines.

Centre right:

Encountering very few Japanese fighters (there was only one major engagement between the Mk VIIIs and the Zeros which the Spitfires won handsomely), most Spits were engaged on bombing and ground attack operations. Here a 500lb bomb is about to be loaded at an airfield in Burma.

Right:

A pleasing air-to-air study of the Mk IXb now with the IWM's collection at Duxford. This was a medium altitude aircraft which performed best between 16,000 and 28,000ft. The Mk IXa went rather too high for me — I never much enjoyed larking around at up to 42,000ft, unable to speak and with neither heat nor cabin pressure.

Above left:
The second of the Mk IX's radiators was used to accommodate the oil cooler and as a radiator for the two-speed, two-stage blower intercooler. The blower engaged and disengaged itself automatically with the usual heart-stopping 'clumps'. This extra radiator evened up the drag and made trimming somewhat easier. The aircraft illustrated is a Mk IXa.

Left:
Another Mk IXa with the Merlin 61 engine showing the longer — about 9in — and slightly higher nose (a bit of a nuisance, this), and the old-type air intake which on later aircraft was moved forward. The radiator flaps were automatic, too, which was a great help as the pilot didn't have to worry so much about the engine temperature. A nice aircraft with a gentle four-bladed airscrew beat, very like the Mk VIII to fly and almost indistinguishable from the Mk XVI.

Above and Right:
The 'works' on a restored Mk IX (it could even be an VIII or a XVI!) in South Africa. The treaded ~~~~~~ ~oth modern and ~~~~~~ ~ ~ a Spit with

THE SPITFIRE Mk XII

Early in 1943, No 41 Squadron learned that it was to be re-equipped with Spitfire Mk XIIs, which came as a great surprise as none of us had ever heard of the aircraft, far less seen one.

All agog to fly one without delay, it took me a whole day to track one down, eventually doing so at the Air Fighting Development Unit at Duxford, a trials unit then commanded by Don Finlay, the celebrated Olympic hurdler and a former commander of No 41 Squadron during the Battle of Britain.

As with my first Mk V, my introduction to the XII was not without incident. First, I had trouble starting the engine; the Mk XII had a Coffman cartridge starter – unlike most other marks of Spit which used a 12V external battery – the trick being to prime the engine correctly before firing the gun as it was not possible to squirt fuel into the cylinders whilst it was turning over. Get it wrong and it wouldn't go, as I was soon to learn as it took me nine embarrassing cartridges to get the big Griffon to work, the Coffman magazine holding only five.

My second mistake was to take-off on the shortest possible run towards the hangars – Duxford was a grass airfield in those days – and being convinced when absolutely committed that I was going to go through the hangar and not over it. Even now I can

Below:
DP845 was used as a test-bed first for the Merlin 20 engine and then for the first Griffon engine of 1,750hp, being referred to variously as a Spitfire Mk III, then a IV and occasionally as the XX.

bring on a rash when I recall the sight of the tiles on that curving hangar roof.

On 23 February 1943 the squadron moved to High Ercall in Shropshire to await the arrival of its new aircraft. As the Spitfire Mk XII was reputedly faster low down than even the Typhoon and was something of a 'hot ship', there was a painful air of smugness abroad in dispersal. Our collective ego was, however, knocked sideways when our first aircraft was delivered by a pretty, pink-cheeked young female in ATA (Air Transport Auxiliary) uniform, who taxied in with a flourish and stepped out as though she had been flying nothing more exciting than a Tiger Moth. The remainder, all delivered by the fair sex, came in ones and twos until we had our full quota of 18.

The Learning Process

Pilot's Notes yet to become available, instruction came in the form of a quick 30-min talk by a junior engineer officer from Group Headquarters. He it was who explained that the Mk XII was the outcome of a dispute between the protagonists of the Rolls-Royce Griffon and those of the Merlin, the latter insisting that the smaller engine could be taken beyond 2,000hp, which would be sufficient to meet the needs of the Spitfire for the foreseeable future.

For them however, the battle apparently had been lost as we had on our hands what was essentially a new aircraft. Originally termed the Spitfire Mk IV, it was first flown in November 1941, the Rolls-Royce Griffon engine then being described by Jeffrey Quill,

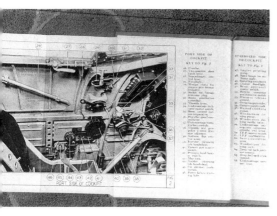

Above:

Left, centre and right view of a Spitfire Mk XII cockpit. All Spitfire cockpits were pretty much the same, this differing from a Mk V's only in detail — the 'stirrup pump' engine primer, the Coffman starter selector, the fuel 'On/Off' cock, and the manual control for the two-speed supercharger. *Crown Copyright*

the principal test pilot of Supermarine, as the direct descendant of the magnificent 'R' type engine which had powered the winning Schneider Trophy seaplanes between 1929 and 1931. He, with other civilian and Service test pilots, had spoken glowingly of the performance of the new Spit and its engine, opinions which some in 41 were disinclined to share when we began to have problems with both the airframe and the engine.

Even so, we started off full of enthusiasm, having been given six weeks to raise our new aircraft and ourselves to full operational status.

The Griffon Engine

The Griffon 3, with which our first Mk XIIs were powered, was substantially different in design. First, the airscrew went round the other way, causing the aircraft to swing to the right on take-off — and right meanly at that! The propeller

itself was much larger and of four blades to absorb the 1,750hp, and the spinner impressively bigger.

Internally, the two-speed, single-stage supercharger, instead of being driven off the rear of the crankshaft, was taken off the airscrew reduction gear at the front of the engine via a long shaft running through the sump. There was one magneto instead of the usual two, housed in a small blister just behind the propeller, and there was said to be a unique oil system, referred to as 'end-feed', a feature we were unable to see and therefore took on trust.

More immediate and visible differences were the 12lb boost instead of the 16lb of our Mk Vs, 2,750rpm instead of the 3,000 we were used to, plus new ejector-type exhausts, which gave the Griffon a harsh, metallic snarl. Gone, too, was our Pan's-pipe whistle! However, to our great satisfaction, we were informed that the old bugbear of the Merlin cutting out under negative 'g' was a thing of the past — no more rich mixture cuts and yards of black smoke for us whenever the noses of our Spits were sharply depressed! Alas, this alleged improvement turned out to be something of a joke. Having started flying, we discovered that not only did our engines cut out under negative 'g', they did so under positive 'g' as well, causing us endless trouble as we could barely make a rate-four turn without having them splutter and cough.

Finally, after some acidic exchanges between the technical staff at Group Headquarters and ourselves, it was decided to bring in an expert from RAE Farnborough and, greatly to our surprise, a tiny, Bohemian-looking lady — a Miss Schilling — arrived at High Ercall astride an ancient and raucous motorbike. From the greasy pocket of an even greasier leather jacket, she produced a handful of restrictors, looking for all the world like thin polo mints, and, disappearing beneath the cowlings of the nearest aircraft, immediately got to work.

Thereafter, it was a tedious and long-winded exercise of trial and error but after some days of noisy experimentation and many take-offs and landings, she finally sorted out our carburettor difficulties.

The Airframe

As No 41 Squadron was the first unit to receive the Mk XIIs, ours were merely converted Mk Vs, fitted with the universal wing but with only two cannons and four machine guns; those of the total batch of 100 aircraft which came later were converted Mk VIIIs, with modified rear ends and retractable tailwheels.

From various sources we heard that on our own aircraft, *this* had been strengthened and *that* had been changed, most of which we accepted on trust as we were far too busy sorting out more immediate engine and operating difficulties. We were told, for example, that an extra 12gal of fuel had been installed in each of the two wing roots, which certainly made sense as at anything like full-bore, with the normal 85gal, our new Spits only had an endurance of about 35min – which was ridiculous. Rather more obvious was a new fuel-contents gauge which was a delayed action affair, taking seemingly endless seconds to produce the information we required – later, an irritating inconvenience when miles into enemy territory.

In order to counteract the effect of the much larger engine and airscrew and the tendency of the aircraft to turn round the propeller rather than the propeller round the aircraft, besides an enlarged tail section, we had a rudder which needed constant retrimming whenever the throttle was moved even a trifle. This was one of the aircraft's least attractive characteristics and a constant source of annoyance as, enjoyment apart, it greatly reduced the aircraft's efficiency as a gun platform.

Because of the extra weight up front and the greater torque, it was found necessary to have the tyres much harder and the port oleo-leg of the undercarriage inflated to a far higher pressure, the aircraft swinging quite hard to the right on its take-off run.

In the cockpit, much was the same other than the Coffman cartridge starter and its procedure, which was a little odd at first, although we soon turned it to our advantage, being able to start a squadron of 12 Spitfires at the drop of a hat – a most impressive sight besides being operationally beneficial. A little different, too, was the ki-gas primer, which was the size of a stirrup-pump, and a single 'on-off' bowden-cable fuel-cock device, which was to cause serious difficulties in the months ahead. Moreover, with one offset radiator – though enlarged – to cope with the bigger engine, we still had the age-old problem of overheating on the ground.

Even so, such differences were merely trifles.

Flying Characteristics

In the air, the Mk XII behaved much like any other Spitfire except that the engine was a good deal rougher than the Merlin – it grumbled rather than buzzed – and the beat of the big four-bladed airscrew was very pronounced. It was about 30mph faster low down than the Mk V for roughly the same engine settings, the nose wagging about like a terrier's tail with any change of power. There being no provision for emergency boost – there was rather too much 'urge', anyway – 9lb was obtained with the throttle at the gate and 12lb beyond it, at which setting a genuine 325mph could be achieved at sea level.

As with earlier Spitfires, the aircraft's maximum performance was obtained at around 18,000ft, where the second stage of the supercharger was engaged manually, using a lever on the left-hand side of the cockpit. In common with all two-speed superchargers, it came in with a slightly worrying 'clump', although we seldom found ourselves using it as, more often than not, we were at 1,800ft rather than 18,000. Moreover, the use of FS gear increased fuel consumption so much that we always remained in MS whenever possible (Fast or Medium Speed).

Although lack of internal fuel obliged us always to fly with a 30gal drop-tank, low down the Mk XII remained remarkably nippy and manoeuvrable, its clipped wings – which were a considerable novelty in the spring of 1943 – adding to the rapidity with which a pilot could up-end a wing, over and above the facility afforded by the metal ailerons. It was pleasant to fly, too, as the nose appeared shorter, the new engine permitting a slight redesign of the front cowling which dropped away towards the propeller. On the debit side, it was noticeably heavier than the Mk V, with a higher stalling speed – and landing speed – and one was always conscious of the whopping great airscrew, the tips of which were all too close to the ground when operating from a rough grass airfield.

Operational Use

In April 1943, No 41 Squadron moved to Hawkinge (Folkestone, Kent), where the operational task was low-level reconnaissance, requiring us to fly single aircraft at sea level along the enemy coast – 'Jim Crow' work, so called – plus various other specialist tasks.

And it was in the reconnaissance role that we suffered our first casualties; one aircraft crashed just short of Hawkinge airfield after a quick and urgent sortie to Flushing in Holland, having suffered

Right:
One of our first Mk XII casualties: this aircraft had an engine failure when returning from a trip to Flushing and crashed on the side of Hawkinge airfield, killing its pilot.

a catastrophic engine failure; the second when one of my flight commanders disappeared off Le Touquet for no apparent reason – no enemy action, no warning, no anything.

These particular losses, occurring as they did within days of our commencing operational duty, caused some sucking of teeth as niggling doubts about the reliability of the Griffon engine were beginning to manifest themselves. Months later, after several more unaccountable losses, it became known that the teleflex control to the fuel tank was coming adrift in the pilot's hand when that unfortunate man, having exhausted his 30gal slipper-tank, was in the act of changing over from drop-tank to mains. Left with his main tanks full but unable to use the fuel therein, he was obliged either to land in enemy territory or fall into the sea.

On a more personal note, I had selected EN237 (EB-V) as my own aircraft and in so doing made a sad

Below:
EB-V, my own Mk XII at Hawkinge in April 1943, and a problem aircraft if ever there was one! One of the earliest Mk XIIs, it did not have the retractable tail-wheel, etc. A 30gal slipper-tank is attached, though barely seen.

mistake, it being one of those rare 'Friday afternoon' Spitfires – in short, a lemon! Over a period of three months, at least one cylinder of the engine would cut out completely after the motor had been running for anything from two to 10min which, when engaged on an operational sortie within 10ft of the sea, was less than amusing. And despite everything being checked, rechecked, adjusted and replaced, continued to do so until the engine was finally removed and sent back to the makers.

My aircraft also possessed another gremlin affecting the 30gal slipper-tank, which we were in the habit of discarding when crossing into enemy territory. On being jettisoned, the tank was supposed to drop down fractionally before moving backwards and impingeing on two lugs which served to tip it forward so that it cartwheeled away from the belly of the aircraft. Alas, not on mine! On two out of every three trips, my tank would impale itself on the lugs, either sticking there (rampant!) and greatly reducing my aircraft's performance, or whipping off sometime later, when it would whirl like a boomerang between those unfortunate members of my squadron who happened to be flying behind me. Not unreasonably, there were bitter complaints from those at the back of the formation, but despite infinite care and many adjustments, a solution was never found by the time I left the unit in the late summer.

Below:
The Focke-Wulf FW190, with which the Mk XII could cope adequately if not easily, the performance of the two types low down being not greatly dissimilar.
RAFM P012132

Performance

In terms of performance, the Mk XII could outdistance a FW190 – which it was obliged to do when operating in the reconnaissance role – and also the Typhoon. The latter was by far the greater threat, as those based at Lympne and Manston were reluctant to accept that the new, square-winged aircraft rushing about the south coast, were anything other than Bf109s! As regards in-fighting, there were few opportunities to test our Mk XIIs capabilities, although we were always confident we could outperform anything the opposition could put up, most encounters resolving themselves into high-speed chases or escapes!

After a brief but unsuccessful attempt to absorb No 41 Squadron into the Biggin Hill wing, which flew Spitfire Mk IXbs – the two types of aircraft were incompatible in terms of performance, particularly endurance – the XIIs were moved down to Friston and employed against tip-and-run raiders attacking Eastbourne, Brighton, and other coastal towns. Unhappily, they were not well suited to Friston, which was merely a lumpy stretch of cow-pasture on the tip of Beachy Head, the result being a series of damaged undercarriages and a number of shorter propellers!

Later still, and recognising that the Mk XII, though performing well, was something of an ugly duckling, the two squadrons equipped with the type – Nos 41 and 91 – joined up at West Hampnett to form a wing. Their role became that of strike fighters operating at 15,000ft and below, usually in the area of Normandy, the Cherbourg peninsula and beyond. Later still, the squadron moved down to the West Country, by which time I had moved on.

Above:
One of the later Mk XIIs showing the redesigned cowling, behind the propeller and the lump housing the forward-placed magneto. All our Spits had the universal 'C' wing with the tips removed, the later model having the Griffon VI engine and not the III or IV. *Rolls-Royce 89.1788.6*

PLACE: **RAF West Hampnett in the Tangmere Sector**

DATE: **July 1943**

Operational instructions for the following day normally arrive at about 9pm in the form of a teleprinted message known as Form 'D' – all 6ft of it! Form 'D' also contains instructions for all other No 11 Group wings and squadrons, so that everyone knows what everyone else is doing. As squadron commander, I usually hang around the Sector Operations Room until it appears.

On this occasion the Form 'D' does not arrive until midnight, by which time I am tired and on edge. I

Below:
Map of the Channel coasts showing flight paths during the incident described in which No 41 Squadron Spitfires and 8th Air Force B-17s were involved.

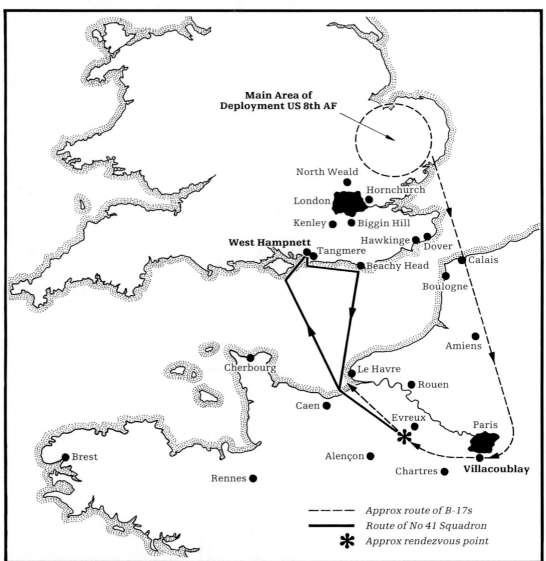

Above:
Typhoons of 266 Squadron. The original code letters of the squadron, UO, were changed to ZD in 1942. At the time of the incident described, this squadron was based at Exeter with sections at Warmwell, in Dorset.

quickly scan the instructions and see that No 41 Squadron will be acting in conjuction with No 91 in providing cover for a formation of American Fortresses returning from a bombing attack on Villacoublay (Paris). There will also be diversionary attacks by several squadrons of Typhoons on enemy airfields in the area of Evreux, all of us fighters crossing the Channel in a single formation at nought feet to thwart enemy radar. Apart from the bombers, about 100 of us will be rendezvousing at Beachy Head well below the height of the cliffs.

There is a mass of other information and instructions: primary objectives, methods of attack, rendezvous points, use of radio, drop-tanks, radio frequencies, and much more besides — the usual stuff. Thus forewarned, to bed.

The following morning, I arrive early to check serviceability and find that No 41 can raise its full quota of 12 aircraft. I watch my flight commanders select their pilots and write down details of the aircraft and people involved on the stateboard. Everyone preparing. Arranging. Making ready. After which — briefing.

The two West Hampnett squadrons usually foregather either in Flying Wing Headquarters or one or other of the two squadron crewrooms. Here, the operation is discussed in detail, the various tasks and objectives clarified. Then the route, formation details, likely enemy response and areas of flak, RT procedures and frequencies, emergencies, weather — the usual string of advice, facts and technicalities, plus a final reminder about emptying pockets and a time check.

The briefing lasts about 30min, watches are set to the second — each pilot has already been issued with a two-guinea watch he *knows* the RAF values infinitely more than him, his Spitfire, or both of them together! — after which everyone disperses, some

laughing, some quiet and thoughtful, some discussing. One hour to take-off

I usually like to be on my own prior to a sortie over the other side. I walk out and check my aircraft carefully, first having a chat with my crew. After which, a clockwise inspection of tyres, panels, fasteners, control surfaces, pitot-head, and finally windscreen and hood, instructing my rigger to give both a final polish.

In particular I check my 30gal slipper-tank, which is always giving trouble, looking carefully to see that the small glass inspection tube connecting tank to fuselage is not damaged and properly in place. Having had one tube broken and my engine stop in mid-air on changeover, I never want that to happen again, especially as on this occasion I shall be changing from mains to reserve at tree-top height.

After that, I arrange the straps of my parachute nestling in its bucket seat so that they are properly laid out and see that the leads from my helmet and face-mask hanging on the control column are securely attached to the radio plug and oxygen supply. My gloves, Mae West, flying boots and the rest, I shall wear, of course, but meanwhile I shall polish and de-mist my goggles — which I do, there and then. Almost surreptitiously I touch the 'secret' compass which forms part of one of my uniform buttons and run my fingers over the escape maps and hacksaw blade concealed in the shoulder pads and lining of my tunic. All there, but what a laugh! The Huns knew every one of these ploys of ours and probably had a hangarful of button compasses and the rest — but we go on carrying them on the off-chance they might come in handy.

I have another word with my fitter and rigger who are watching a little apprehensively, and park the maps of southern England and France I am carrying in the small map case in the cockpit. Plus a short list of courses and precise timings written on a piece of paper which I hope I shall have the time to destroy if I am shot down and captured. The wing leader will be in front on this occasion but I would need to have my own cribs should anything go wrong or the wing split up, which is more than likely should there be a fight.

After another circuit of my aircraft, I make a final check of the gun-panel fasteners; as my Mk XII has the Mk V universal wing, my two cannons are now belt-fed with 120 rounds each gun and my four machine guns with 300 rounds apiece. All fasteners secure, I run my fingers over the linen-covered ports of the machine guns and the two plastic gaiters of the cannons — they will all be off in a flash if and when the guns are fired.

I glance at my watch: 30min to go. Other pilots are climbing over their Spits, preparing their aircraft and their equipment. Time for the 700s and authorisation book.

The list of pilots and aircraft already entered, I sign in the allotted space for each of the 11 who is accompanying me. Then an additional signature for my own flight, after which I pick out the Form 700 for EN237. I read it carefully. Sixty-five hours on the engine now with a whole string of complaints about the obscure ignition problem that has been plaguing me ever since I took over the aircraft, all of which have been investigated — it SAYS! Also the perennial slipper-tank difficulty — has that too been sorted out? I read on and see that adjustments have been made — for the sixth time. Well, we'd see!

I run my finger across the appropriate columns — fuel, oil, radio, oxygen, all the signatures — I sign at the end of the line and have a word with the sergeant who is watching not without concern. I tell him that should my aircraft let me down I will return to haunt him and he grins and makes some suitable response in an Oxbridge accent. In civilian life he is a floor supervisor in the gentlemen's department of Moss Bros in Covent Garden where he wears a morning suit every working day of the week.

Ten minutes to go. I button up my Mae West, tie the tapes between my legs and check around my person for the things I should, and should not have! After which, out to my aircraft.

My Spit, beautiful to look at, its elongated spinner and four-bladed airscrew almost too big for the fuselage. Shining. And colourful in its camouflage green and brown, its duck-egg blue nose and tail band, its proud letters EB-V and yellow, blue and red circles on fuselage and wing. As are all the others, in a longish, zig-zag line — the Huns don't attack our airfields these days and dispersal is not the 'must' it used to be.

I climb in and settle down. Parachute harness first, with the lead to my dinghy. Then the Sutton harness — I wriggle about and try the release mechanism before locking it again. Then, my helmet, mask and goggles, the goggles being finally pushed away from my nose — I would pull them down later. After which, my gloves — all three pairs.

After a careful cockpit check during which I set my elevator and rudder trimmers and tighten the friction device on my throttle and airscrew pitch lever, I finally clip on my face-mask, check the flow

of oxygen, and sit. And wait. Noting that 11 heads are turned in my direction. I glance at my watch and, as an afterthought, set our first course from Beachy Head to approximately Le Havre on my compass. Finally, as the seconds tick by, I unscrew my 'stirrup-pump' ki-gas primer, give four juicy squirts, then screw it back into position.

I check my watch again and, as the second-hand moves in minute staccato hops to its appointed mark, raise my arm.

Instantly, there is a series of muffled reports, hisses, and bursts of engine exhaust as eleven Griffon engines explode into life, the Spitfires, individually, climbing against their chocks, blue smoke from the Coffman starters rising in a miniature cloud before being swirled away by a forest of flashing airscrew blades.

My own engine warm, it starts immediately with its customary snarl and, waving away the chocks, I taxi briskly away with a surge of power, anxious to reach the far end of the grass airfield before the big Griffon begins to overheat.

Bouncing and rocking, all 12 of No 41 Squadron waddle into the distance like an untidy gaggle of geese whilst, on the far side of the aerodrome, the aircrews of No 91 dissolve into blurs as their engines

Below:
Spitfire Mk XIIs of No 41 Squadron in something resembling battle formation.

are started. In front, my thoughts are only of my engine temperature and the business of getting off the ground quickly, although automatically, my hands and eyes are going through the drill of preparation.

At the far end we turn, clumsily, and assemble in a broad vee of three fours. Every masked face looking impassively in my direction. Radios on but silent in accordance with our briefing instructions.

When ready, I raise my arm and motion everyone forward like the 7th Cavalry. We all begin to roll, trundling across the grass. Slowly. Carefully. Bouncing. Rocking. Sorting ourselves out.

Then, I am gathering speed and, first with +4 then with 6lb boost on the gauge, race ahead, the grass tumbling and streaking beneath. Now 7lb — more than enough — and I am aware of the powerful tendency of my Spit to swing to the right. Lifting now — touching — touching — and AWAY! My engine raging at 2,750 revs, my followers up their gates, hanging on. A quick glance left and right — the whole formation airborne, swaying and dipping. After which, the wheels, drumming initially, then a touch of brake followed by a tiny 'thump' and a red light.

Lifting over the hangars now, people in groups gawping and shielding their ears against the bedlam of noise, followed by a flatish turn to the left — at all costs must not climb much above hangar height. My aircraft riding the jolting upcurrents and everyone streaming in pursuit, cutting the corners and heading for the line of the nearby coast.

Ducking down to tree-top height, I close my hood, which runs forward and locks with an audible snap, reduce to 2lb boost and bring back my revs to a fraction under 2,400 — my engine has a smooth spot there. Roads, houses, trees, streak beneath. And people with upturned pink faces. My gauges all normal, I decide to go on to reserve.

At less than 50ft, this operation is always fraught with danger — if the system doesn't work, any one of us could be a goner within seconds. I bend to my right to switch on the slipper-tank of 30gal, then turn off the main tank supply, pushing down the single teleflex control in front of me. A fleeting moment of suspense but everything works and I relax.

I straighten my Spit, settle down and fly in the direction of Beachy Head with 265 on the clock, adjusting the throttle slightly to keep the needle of the ASI steady on its mark. My aircraft bouncing and rocking in the summer convection currents, I keep an eagle eye open for pylon wires and tall trees. Thus far, fine! My engine is behaving itself and no one has uttered a word. A thin line of sand and houses approaches then streams diagonally beneath, after-which we are over the sea.

It takes about seven minutes to reach Beachy Head and as I see the white cliffs in the distance, I study the second-hand on my cockpit clock knowing full

Left:
A group of Mk XIIs over Sussex in early 1944. No 41 Squadron was at Friston at the time, on the tip of Beachy Head.
Rolls-Royce 89.1788.2

well what will happen — eight squadrons will arrive at precisely the same moment, all below 50ft and from different directions. Ninety-six fighter aircraft! And chaos, if we are not very careful. My squadron behind and alongside in three compact echeloned lines of four, know it, too, and are wary, waiting for a sudden and dramatic change of direction.

All the time, the sea streaking beneath, like a fast-moving roller blind. And not a word being spoken.

We arrive, and it takes one complete turn below cliff-top height to sort ourselves out, Spitfires and Typhoons alike. I thank God I am flying a Spit as the Napier Sabre engines in the Typhoons are notoriously unreliable. After which, barely above the waves and in a vast tilting phalanx, we set course.

Having made the crossing many times before, I am well aware of what is ahead. At 265 indicated, it is about 20min before we pass to the right of Le Havre and a further minute or two before we cross into France around Deauville. The coast is low-lying there and we can usually get away without too much flak. Enemy aircraft I can cope with but not flak, which I definitely do not like, having been hit very early on in my career.

Meanwhile, I concentrate on the aircraft ahead, pay particular attention to the waves racing a mere 20ft beneath, and cock an interested eye at several Typhoons to my right, one of which is flying so close to the water that I feel sure it will hit it sooner or later.

And it *does*! There is a sudden explosion of spray and the aircraft rears into the air like a winged grouse, after which, to my astonishment, the pilot carries on, though at a more respectable distance. I have no feelings about the incident other than irritation; if the silly blighter wants to fly into the sea, that's his business.

More than half-way across, I check around my cockpit. gunsight 'ON' — I adjust the pink graticules to the proper brightness and set the range and wingspan bars at 200yd and 40ft — for 109s and 190s, naturally — slip my gun-button to 'FIRE',

heighten my seat in order to see just that little bit better, and lower my goggles. Safety harness free, then locked — CLICK! Everything set!

After which, off to my left — land! I increase my boost to around 6lb and revs to 2,600, knowing full well that my formation will be doing the same. As the coastline races towards us, we all prepare. Then, with a flash of sand and salt-flat, we are away — throttles to the gate and noses soaring skywards as we haul our aircraft into a steep climb, the speed falling away rapidly until we have barely 200 on the clock. Within moments and with engines raging, we are at 7,000ft and still climbing steeply, the whole coastline of Normandy spread out below. Soon we are approaching 10,000ft and beginning to flatten out.

At this point we have arranged to shed our slipper-tanks. I waggle my wings in a series of exaggerated movements and No 41 spreads out into a wide battle formation. No need for radio silence now; we are in position and receiving information on the enemy from Sector back home. But, for the moment, the tanks.

I pass the word and select main tanks 'ON' by bringing up the lever on the teleflex control in front of my knees, almost simultaneously reaching down to switch off the fuel from the slipper-tank and pull the jettison handle. There are slight goings-on underneath, followed by a brief shimmy and a metallic thud — which is all too familiar! GOD not again! The tank has come off but has stuck! I mouth unprintable words before rocking my aircraft violently in an effort to dislodge the brute, but no such luck — it is jammed. Solid!

I force myself to concentrate on the job on hand. I am 10 miles into France at 12,000ft and Caen is a grey smudge behind me and to my right. My aircraft is buffeting a bit but flying reasonably enough. Do I turn for home with my number two, or carry on? Strictly against the rules, I choose the latter course of action and pray that I am right. The 'Tiffies' have long since departed so that we two Spitfire squadrons are alone, well spread out and racing

towards the south with throttles well advanced and 270 on the clock.

A small but urgent voice from Sector on channel 'B' of our radios. Playmates *(Friendly bombers or other aircraft)* are 30 miles south-east, apparently, and turning north, angels 14! And several groups of bogeys, 20 plus and more, are in our area and at various heights. With my slipper-tank sticking out like a sore thumb, that's *all* I need! We turn left and begin to search, still racing. Flak begins to stain the sky to our left and ahead but not dangerously so. I judge that Alençon is in front and to my right; we are 30 miles from the coast and totally committed.

Nothing much happens for a minute or more as we search for the Fortresses. Then tension heightens rapidly as someone reports four bandits seven-o'clock and above, which, because they are behind me, I do not see immediately. I turn, hard, and in the act of changing direction, the slipper-tank flies off and it is as though my aircraft is released from a spring. The buffeting disappears and everything is smooth again. Thank God!

But God is not that charitable! Within a minute, my engine begins to stutter — the old ignition trouble again — one cylinder cutting out completely so that everything begins to shake, not a lot, but enough for me to wish I were over England and not within spitting distance of Paris.

Then much more flak in the distance and suddenly a thick wedge of slow-moving Fortresses coming in our direction.

We are at 13,000ft and the bombers a little above, several straggling. Sector is warning us again of more bandits in our area but I do not see them. Mild confusion with everyone in a wide curve and climbing. What now? I swiftly note that we have

Above:
B-17 Flying Fortresses of the 381st Bomb Group leave streams of condensing vapour as they roar towards their objective. This was the group that No 41 Squadron occasionally escorted. *USAF*

Left:
Flak bursts close to a B-17 of the 381st. This demonstrates yet another hazard to both bomber and fighter pilots. *USAF*

been airborne almost 50min and don't want to go much further into France, thank you very much! My fuel gauge is registering some extraordinary amount so I give up looking at it.

Then more chatter on the RT and a small group of strange-looking aircraft streams past in a fast-moving line. I turn instinctively and begin to give chase. They are FW190s and going like the clappers — downward and away. Several others are to my left and above and I change direction towards them — hard — but they climb and sweep silently and swiftly over my head.

Now there are two more about 800yd away, slanting towards me and looking very unfriendly. As I watch almost dispassionately, white rods of tracer reach out in my direction to disappear somewhere astern. I pull around so violently that my Spit shudders in a near stall and almost groans. The two 190s flash underneath, for a moment in plain view

Below:
A FW190 under attack at about 120yd. With strikes like these, the attacking aircraft ran a grave risk of being damaged by flying debris.

and so close that the blunt nose and black crosses of one of them are clearly visible. I follow, my engine raging and shaking, becoming suddenly smooth again as a puff of black smoke flicks from my exhausts signifying a miraculous clearance. Glory be!

Heartened by my engine's magical recovery and wildly elated, I follow, pumping my controls like some biblical drawer of water, trying to get the second of the two 190s into my windscreen and sight. But the blighter is going like a dart, streaking away to my left and diving. I cut the corner, gaining a little and pulling hard. I sense that we are going south and don't like it very much as the mass of bombers and other Spits are now astern of me and heading in the other direction.

The Hun now 500-600yd away — too far for a decent shot. My number two should be around somewhere but I can't see him and don't relish the idea of being on my own so far into France and at 8,000ft.

Almost as a gesture, I fire. My two cannons thump and jerk and a stream of spark-flecked tracer twists into the distance from my four Brownings which are loaded consecutively with ball, armour-piercing, and De Wilde (De Wilde ammunition — a type of incendiary). Two seconds' worth — just to show willing and to put the wind up the blighter.

The result, almost predictably, is NIL! No flashes or obvious strikes. The 190s continue on their dramatic downward curve and I pull up and climb steeply away, feeling nakedly alone and wanting to get back among my mates. Far away, the sky is still stained with faint brown traces of flak and I head in that direction, praying that I shall not be bounced again en route.

Then relief: the comforting, detached voice of Sector. Some of the Fortresses have been hit and may have to ditch. We are to stay with them and give all available assistance until they are over the Channel. Stay with them! All I have to do now is FIND them!

With my number two, who suddenly surges into view on my left, I fly north and eventually spot the main bomber formation in the distance. There is one Fortress well below the rest and I deduce this to be one of the victims. I fly alongside to boost the spirits of the chaps within and go over to channel 'D', which is the distress frequency. Sure enough, the American crew are not at all happy and make no bones about broadcasting their predicament. I fly straight and level for some moments and carefully examine my slow-motion petrol gauge, noting that I am well into the fuel in my bottom tank. Sufficient for 40min or so at the outside — and I'm still 100 miles from home and 15 miles into France with a shadowing job on my hands. If we are attacked now, we will be forced to retaliate and obliged to leave the Forts or drop into the sea ourselves. Why don't these ruddy Spits carry a bit more fuel?

Despite many warnings from Sector and much chatter on the RT, the Huns inexplicably leave us alone and I am one of a group which shepherds the limping Fortress across the French coast at less than 5,000ft and out into the Channel. At which point, my engine begins to miss again, this time so manifestly in earnest that I have real fears that I shall be in the water myself, with or without assistance from the Hun!

A little later, seriously short of fuel and with most of 41 collected around me, I fly off northwards at little more than 2,000ft. Sector passes the information that an air-sea rescue Walrus is on its way. For the Fortress, I wonder, or for me?

After an age, the cliffs of the Isle of Wight appear and we all veer off to the right, huddled in our usual formation of three fours line-astern. Crossing into Sussex, we dive gently towards West Hampnett and roar over the airfield at 500ft and 300mph — our 'erks' like to see their own squadron return in one piece and put on a performance!

We circle and sort ourselves out. In 41, we always land on the grass in 'vics' of four with Guard's Brigade precision, and woe betide any junior pilot who overtakes his leader during the approach or on the ground!

We approach on slow-motion finals, like matrons with lifted skirts, and touch down, our Spits ballooning gracefully over the uneven grass with crackling exhausts and tiny puffs of blue smoke. All 12 have landed before I, as leader, begin to taxi in.

We climb out stiffly. Someone is loudly complaining about my drop-tank coming off and nearly crowning him. No one lost, it seems, but not very much achieved either, although the Fortress looked as though it might make it back to the English coast.

Finally, the heat of battle evaporating, we disperse. Another day another dollar! But that was war, wasn't it? Lots of tedious waiting and hanging about punctuated by bouts of frenetic activity and excitement.

I walk back to my aircraft, now silent and innocently docile. There are 10gal of fuel remaining, I note. Two more minutes with those 190s and I would have been paddling home in my dinghy and not standing here dry and in one piece. If only we had another 30-or-so gallons!

On the Form 700, I write in caustic terms about my engine and slipper-tank problems. I discuss the matter with a forlorn-looking engineer officer and later with the station's Chief Technical Officer. About the Griffon, they are in despair and agree that I should have a new engine. As regards my drop-tank, well, they would just have to go on trying, wouldn't they?

Later in the month I get a new engine but the slipper-tank difficulty remains unresolved.

Some Spitfires were like that. Not all — just a few!

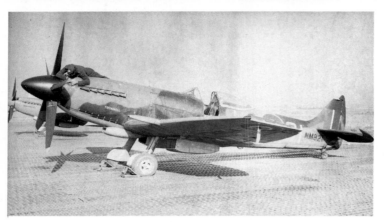

Left:
A fighter recce Mk XIV with the then newish teardrop hood and redesigned rear fuselage. The oblique camera can be seen just above above the port navigation light. The aircraft was pleasant enough to fly though much rougher and more brutal than the average Merlin-engined Spit. Note the PSP-pierced steel planking — forming the hard standing.

Centre left:
I flew the PR XIX a lot in 1946 and quite liked it as it had masses of fuel and a pressurised cockpit, although some didn't. From the bulge just below the port exhaust stubs, this one did.

Below:
Three Spitfire Mk XXs of No 60 Squadron fitted with 60lb rockets, operating in Malaya in 1948.

Above right:
A smart-looking Mk F22 with the new-look wing, enlarged tail and outer wheel flaps. *Flight 19505s*

Centre right:
This F22 is fitted with a non-standard contrarotating prop. *Vickers 5067-G*

Below:
I have to include PK312 which, despite its handsome appearance, was probably the most miserable Spitfire I ever flew. The prototype F22, it was pretty tired when it arrived at Boscombe Down, where I flew it in 1946 on a series of stability trials, never having a dull moment in the process.

Above:

Finally the Spiteful, a beautiful-looking aircraft with a laminar flow wing. I flew a Seafang — which was the naval version of the Spiteful — which had powered ailerons, then quite new to me. I can remember little about it except that there was a tiny dead spot in the middle in which I could waggle the control column without anything happening. The end of a long and glorious line, alas!